RODDY BOY

Christopher Harnedy

ISBN: 145654179X
ISBN-13: 9781456541798

Robbery, Assault and Battery

I had never dreamed the last six months of my high school career would be filled with so much drama. I remember a tagline from a TV commercial that stated, "You can't make this stuff up." All of what happened to me during a six-month span from January to June 1988 seems quite far-fetched, even for Hollywood. But, alas, all of what I'm about to recount did happen.

My roller coaster ride started with a sojourn to the St. George Library. I had just finished perusing through old microfilm newspaper articles at the library, and I was on my way to the nearby ferry terminal to catch the homeward bound bus. The early evening February air was bitterly cold, and I cursed myself for not wearing a hat. My ears were ringing and I had only been outside for just two minutes. My long brown hair, parted down the middle, cascaded to my shoulders, but hair covering the ears was of minimal protection against the winter chill.

As I made my way toward the steps that ran alongside stately Staten Island Borough Hall, I was suddenly knocked to the ground. I landed hard on my left wrist, and it bent back. A shooting pain engulfed my lower left arm. Before I could react to what was happening around me, I felt the sharp kicks of boots all over me, with voices shouting, "Get his fuckin' wallet! Get his fuckin' wallet!" The kicks were swift.

It was hard for me to determine my attackers' numbers. There were at least two, and it was difficult to get a look at them. A few of those brutal kicks landed on my head and face, causing me to lose consciousness.

I couldn't recall a whole lot right after the attack. What I did remember while slipping in and out of consciousness on the ground was the voice of a woman above me, asking me if I was okay.

Alertness came to me the next morning as I was lying in my hospital bed at Bayley Seton Hospital. A partition was separating me from an older patient who was punctuating the air with moans and groans. God only knows what was wrong with him; I was preoccupied with my own feeble state. My Aunt Jane came into the hospital room, tears streaming down her cheeks. "I'm so glad ye alive, son," she said in her inimitable Scottish burr. Aunt Jane had been in the country at least 33 years, and she still hadn't lost her accent. Her hair was for the most part still dark brown for her age, and her eyes were chestnut brown. Her cheeks were rosy, and for a middle-aged woman she was still hearty and fresh-faced. Even though she smoked, there were very few wrinkles on her face. She gave me a warm embrace, but I gasped in pain from the hug. Those attackers really did give me a beating. I was hurting all over.

"Oh God," Aunt Jane said, pulling back in horror. "I forgot. The doctor says ye have cracked ribs. I shouldn't have hugged ye." She settled for giving me a pat on the head and a peck on the cheek.

Even that pat on the head stung a little. "What the hell happened to me?" I asked.

"You were mugged, son," my aunt explained. "Vicious animals tried to kill ye and leave ye for dead. Do ye remember anything at all?"

I tried to recollect, but only the mental images of dark-clothed figures and the heavy boots kicking at me came to mind.

"I don't remember anything except getting knocked to the ground and the yelling above me to get my wallet," I answered groggily.

"Ye didn't get a look at any of them?"

"No, Aunt Jane. I didn't even know what was happening."

"How much money did you have on ye, Roddy?"

"Just 20 dollars."

"All for that! It's a lousy shame what is happening to this city. It used to be Staten Island was the safest borough. No more. You'd expect this sort of thing to happen in Brooklyn or the Bronx, but not here. Why did ye have to go to that library? There are other libraries. Why not New Dorp or Dongan Hills? Why St. George? You know that's not a good neighborhood."

"I like that library, Aunt Jane."

"Do ye like it enough to get killed?" she retorted. "Don't walk around there at night again, unless ye like having your noggin used as a football."

I didn't want to explain to Aunt Jane that I was doing research on my parents. She wouldn't have understood it. "Let sleeping dogs lie," she would say. It was true that my parents hadn't been part of my life for a long time, but any kid whose parents died on him would be curious.

The Detective

Aunt Jane was in and out of the hospital that Saturday, running errands. I spent all of that day in the hospital bed with that damned IV sticking in my right arm, watching *Godzilla* movies on the local TV station, WWOR. It is safe to say that hospital food is dreadful and inedible. Swanson TV dinners tasted better than this slop. However, the nurse attending to my needs, a middle-aged black woman, was very attentive and nice.

It was sometime during the early afternoon when I received a visit from a stout man in a bland business suit. He held up his police badge to identify himself.

"Roddy McPherson?"

"Yeah?"

"Hi, my name is Detective Henessey. I'm with the assault victims division of the NYPD. How are you feeling today?"

"Like a train ran over me." That answer came to me very easily.

"I can see that, and I'm sorry. Now, I'm going to be asking you a few questions. Did you get a look at the men who did this?"

I shook my head no.

The detective wasn't going to settle for that nod as an answer. "Kid, I really need you to work with me. This is serious. I can't get these guys off the street unless you do. This is not the first time this has happened in that area. It's been going on for the past month. Now, can you tell me anything?"

"I was walking from the library to the ferry terminal by Borough Hall. The next thing I know, I fell to the ground hard on my wrist. Then I see these boots kicking at me and these voices above me, yelling, 'Get his fuckin' wallet, get his fuckin' wallet.' And after that, I lost consciousness."

"And you didn't get a look at the men that did this to you?" Detective Henessey pressed further.

"No, sir," I answered wearily. I wished this guy would just leave already. Hadn't my Aunt Jane just interrogated me about this a few hours earlier? "It all happened so fast."

The detective was not giving up. "Surely you must have gotten a glimpse at these men."

"No, detective." I was becoming aggravated. "All I saw were boots above me kicking at me and those voices yelling above me. As you can tell, some of those kicks landed on my head and face."

There was no doubting what I had just said. My face was black and blue all over. My eyes resembled those of a raccoon. And along with the black and blue were cuts and scrapes. Those guys thought they were playing soccer. It was astonishing my head was still attached to my body. I had had to close my eyes; otherwise they would have kicked those out.

"Did the voices sound black, Hispanic?"

I shook my head wearily. "I don't know detective, I just don't know."

"Surely you must have gotten a glimpse of these men. You shouldn't be withholding information from me. These men are dangerous and they left you for dead!"

"Look!" I exploded. "I'm telling you the truth, and I don't know what the hell you want me to say. If I saw these men, I'd identify them, but I didn't!"

The detective finally sensed I was telling him the truth and that he was further agitating me. "Okay, son, just take it easy. But if you happen to remember anything, don't hesitate to give me a call. Here's my card."

Detective Henessey placed his business card on my night table and left the room.

A Gentler Kind of Visitor

"Ye have to expect him to ask ye those questions," Aunt Jane said as she sat in the chair on my right side. "I find it hard to believe ye didn't get a look at these thugs either."

This was all too much. Now my own aunt was doubting me. "Why are you taking his side? Doesn't anyone believe me, Goddamnit!"

"Watch ye mouth!" my aunt chided me. "I told ye never to take the Lord's name in vain. Too much riffraff is hanging around at your school, and you're starting to talk like them."

"I'm sorry, Aunt Jane, but why are you taking that detective's side? I'm telling you the truth. I wish I could catch those bastards myself. Everybody is treating me like I'm the criminal."

"I believe ye, Roddy," my aunt affirmed as she placed a hand on my right shoulder. "I wish ye would have gotten a better look at these thugs, because they're going to hurt someone else or, God forbid, kill someone."

An attractive woman I had estimated to be in her 20s, tall and slender, walked into my drab hospital room. She was decked out in a leather jacket, gray sweater, black jeans and boots. Her hair was red, cut spiky short on top, barely touching the ears, and coming down in the back just past her collar. She had a radiant smile and a twinkle in her blue eyes that helped accentuate her square, regal face. She was holding a plate of chocolate chip cookies wrapped in cellophane.

"Hi," announced the young woman. "I hope I'm not disturbing anything."

"Hello, lass," my aunt greeted the woman. "Why don't ye come over and sit?"

The woman declined. "Oh no, Mrs. McPherson. I'm fine. You sit."

"Roddy, this is the lass who found you in the street," my aunt announced. Her name is Brenda."

Brenda offered me her hand to shake. I took it wearily. "I am so glad you are going to be all right," she said. "I thought you were dead when I saw you out on the street. How are you feeling?"

My ribs were cracked, the top of my head felt as if was pushed in and my left wrist was badly sprained but thankfully not broken. My face resembled a busted grapefruit. Quite surprisingly, my nose was left unscathed. "I wouldn't call it living, but it will do," I joked.

Brenda shook her head sadly. "This is so disgusting. I really hope the cops catch these bastards."

"I don't think so," my aunt said grimly. "The mugging happened so fast, Roddy never got a look at those animals."

"That is such a shame," Brenda said, nodding her head again in sadness. "The crime rate in this city is out of control. You really have to be careful nowadays."

"'Tis a shame, lass," my aunt muttered. "It's getting so ye can no longer walk out the door. I wish this Mayor Koch would do something about the crime. It's out of hand!"

"How long does Roddy have to be in here?" Brenda asked Aunt Jane.

"They're releasing him tomorrow afternoon. It's a good thing school is not in session. He can rest up without missing any classes."

"That wouldn't be so bad," I said. I hated school with a passion. I never cared for most of the teachers and disliked many in my age group.

"He's like every other kid nowadays," Aunt Jane explained. "For crying out loud, I wish I could be in school again."

"I'm in school," Brenda joked. "I teach at Normand High."

"Oh, really?" Aunt Jane's eyes brightened. "Roddy goes to school there. What do ye teach?"

"I teach English."

"Roddy, do ye know Brenda from the school?" Aunt Jane inquired.

I looked at Brenda intently, and I didn't remember ever seeing her face in the three and a half years I had been attending that institution. I was entering the final semester of my high school career, and why was it that I had never seen her before? I would have remembered that pretty face.

It was almost as if Brenda sensed my confusion, and she cleared up the matter. "I'm only starting this semester. I've been teaching in Brooklyn the last six years."

"Praise to heaven," my aunt said. "Ye must really be glad yer out of there. That whole borough is a ghetto."

"It wasn't that bad, Mrs. McPherson, although I'm looking forward to the quiet here."

"I'm sure Roddy would have remembered yer face," Aunt Jane said. "He's a teenage boy, and how can teenagers ever forget pretty faces?"

"That's very nice of you to say that," Brenda said, blushing.

"Are ye from Staten Island?" my aunt asked.

"I'm a native Islander, born and raised. I grew up in Stapleton. Now I live in the apartments overlooking Silver Lake Park."

"Are you Scottish?"

"I'm half Irish, half Scottish on my mom's side," Brenda answered. "Her last name is McKellar."

"There are still some of us left," my aunt exclaimed. "There's not too many of us in the city." This comment was alluding to the lack of Scottish in New York City. Aunt Jane was right; I didn't know of too many people of Scottish descent living in New York City. The majority of people, especially here on Staten Island, were of Italian descent, not Scottish.

My aunt continued on with the conversation. "I lived in Bay Ridge for five years. My husband and I immigrated there from Scotland 28 years ago. Five years later, my husband and I moved to the Island. I've been in Rosebank ever since. Roddy is originally from the Bronx, and he came to live with us when he was a wee child. His parents died young on him. And his uncle just passed away last spring. So, it's just him and meself."

"I'm so sorry, Mrs. McPherson, and you too, Roddy," Brenda said sincerely.

"Things happen that are not always under yer control, Brenda. You have to move on," my aunt said stoically. I know it had been especially hard on my aunt when my Uncle Harry passed on, but she really hid a lot. She was tough that way, but I'm sure if I had caught her in private moments, her pain and grief would show.

Aunt Jane checked the time on her watch. "Oh dear, I've got to run, Roddy. I have to get over to the butcher to pick up roast beef dinner, yer favorite. Brenda, would ye like to join us for dinner tomorrow night?"

"Oh, no, I couldn't, Mrs. McPherson," Brenda politely demurred. "That is a very sweet offer, but no thank you."

"Why not, dear? It's the least I could do for ye after ye helped my nephew."

"You don't owe me anything, Mrs. McPherson."

"Oh, will ye please come?" my aunt insisted. "Ye don't have any school to worry about, unless you have a date. Why not bring him too?"

Brenda laughed. "No, I don't have a date, but I'll come if it isn't too much trouble."

"Don't be silly, dear; I offered."

Aunt Jane gave Brenda our home address. "We'll see you at 6." And then she turned to me and gave me a peck on the cheek. "Bye, love. I'll be back later."

Brenda and I were left alone, but there were no awkward pauses. She was a very comfortable person to talk to.

"Do you like chocolate chip cookies?" Brenda asked. "I hope you do, because I baked a whole bunch."

"Are you kidding? I love them. The food sucks here, and I'm starving," I proclaimed.

Brenda laughed. "I know what you mean. A few years ago, I had my tonsils removed at St. Vincent's Medical Center, and their food was lousy too."

"Can I have one?" I asked, motioning for the cookies.

"Sure." Brenda unwrapped the plate and gave me one. My body was hurting all over, but my mouth worked fine. The cookies were moist and chewy the way I liked them. "This is good. Can I have another one?"

"My pleasure," Brenda laughed. "So, what kind of English course are you taking this semester?"

"Creative writing."

"Oh, how cool is that!" Brenda exclaimed happily. "You'll be in my class."

I smiled. A class with a teacher who appeared to be likable. I hadn't liked too many teachers. Nor were they so fond of me. Perhaps it was because I was close-mouthed in the day and tried to blend in with scenery of the classroom.

"That's good," I said. "Most teachers don't like me."

"Oh no," she said with a frown. "Why not?"

"Because I'm shy and quiet. Teachers hate that."

"I have no problems with that whatsoever. All I ask is that you do the assignments. I won't pick on you for being shy and quiet."

"Okay."

"Do you enjoy writing?" Brenda asked.

"I keep a journal. I wouldn't call myself a writer. I'm not that good. But it comes to me easily."

"Well, we'll have to see if it's not good. But we'll work on this," Brenda assured me.

"Great."

"Listen, we're going to talk more tomorrow night. I'm looking forward to this. It was a pleasure meeting you. I'm sorry it had to be under these circumstances. Rest up and feel better, Roddy."

Brenda touched my hand as she said that and walked out of the room. That little visit made up for the obnoxiousness of the detective's visit.

The Family Gathering

"He suffered a concussion from those kicks. His wrist is broken and a few of his ribs are cracked. It's a wonder he wasn't killed," Aunt Jane explained over the course of dinner. I sat uncomfortably, but it didn't stop me from devouring the plate of roast beef and mashed potatoes all slathered in gravy.

This wasn't lost on Aunt Jane. "At least it hasn't affected his appetite none," she remarked in front of all the guests.

Among the guests were my Uncle Tim and Aunt Beth, along with my cousins: 14-year-old Kimberly and 11-year-old Scott. That group was from nearby Cranford, New Jersey. And then there was Brenda, my hero. It was amazing how well she was getting on with everyone at the table. You would have thought she was part of our family. I wasn't particularly thrilled with all these people coming over, but I eventually grew to enjoy the company. It was nice to be fawned over, but Brenda became the center of attention. She had an easy-going, engaging personality. Questions were directed at her, and I thought they were a bit on the personal side.

"How long have you been a teacher?"

"Were you ever married?"

"Are you dating anyone?"

"Where do you live?"

Brenda handled all inquiries good-naturedly and graciously. In the course of a few hours, I learned quite a bit about her. I already knew about her being a Staten Island native and that her background was Scottish/Irish. And that she was living in an apartment off of Silver Lake Park. Well, she actually told us that night she was sharing it with a girlfriend. Brenda had been teaching for more than six and a half years. As she mentioned to my aunt and myself, she started teaching just last semester at my high school. She was not yet 29, but she looked five years younger and really fresh-faced. Brenda was once married but had been divorced for two years.

"It seems like ages ago, and it's better that way. I'd like to forget it." No one at the table pressed her on the issue, but I felt bad for the woman. She must have been sorry she ever came to the house.

My cousin Kimberly remarked to Brenda, "You really seem like a nice teacher. Can you come to my school?"

"No, come to *my* school," Scott chimed in. "My teachers are mean!"

"You're really building up a fan club," Aunt Beth remarked to Brenda.

Between dinner and dessert, I decided to lie down on the living room couch. Kimberly and Scott were glued to the TV set watching the Nickelodeon network.

Brenda came over to the recliner next to me and engaged me in conversation.

"How are you holding up?" she asked.

"I'm still in pain, but I'm glad I'm home," I replied.

"It's going to take some time to heal. At least you have a week to rest up before classes start. Are you looking forward to it?"

"No," I answered point blank. I told her I never had felt comfortable in school. I was just too shy and quiet. I never got along with most other kids and I found it tough going with teachers as well. Perhaps some teachers weren't enamored with a kid not participating in their discussions, but I felt I never had anything to say, and I never wanted to come across as foolish in my answers.

"I'm going to help you overcome this shyness," Brenda announced. "I was like you myself when I was your age." I didn't believe her for one minute. "No way, no way. You don't seem like you're shy."

"Yes I was, Roddy," Brenda pointed out to me. "I was a wallflower when I was a teenager. I didn't grow out of it until my senior year. I had help from a real nice teacher. She taught creative writing, and it was in her class I began to express myself. I always had teachers who were verbally abusive to me. Math teachers were particularly hard on me. I always had trouble with the subject. Why couldn't they see I needed help? That abuse affected my confidence so much, it extended to other classes. I was painfully shy. But that creative writing teacher I had, bless her, helped me so much in my senior year, I gained more confidence in myself and I began to assert myself better. It was because of her that I became a teacher."

"Because you wanted to be like her?" I asked.

"Yes, I did, but I also wanted to become the kind of teacher who would help students, not belittle or berate them. I was in your position once, so, yes, I know how it feels to be alienated."

"And you're going to help me?" I wondered. "How?"

"Don't worry about it. Just rest for now. You'll find out soon enough."

To be truthful, I wasn't particularly concerned about school at that point. I was more concerned about devouring my share of Brenda's world-beating chocolate chip cookies. The two aunts were setting up the table for dessert, and I was eagerly awaiting getting my hands on a few of those mouth-watering cookies.

Rob and the Record Shop

That week before the start of the school semester was rather slow and dull. All I did was sit around and watch MTV. My big excitement would be on Saturdays, when I worked in an East Greenwich Village record shop appropriately called the Record Den, since it was run out of a cellar. But due to my battered condition at the time, I had to miss work that Saturday. It would be the second Saturday in a row I missed working at the Den, since the previous Saturday was spent recuperating in the hospital. My aunt had called the Record Den earlier in the week, informing Rob, the owner of the shop, of my condition. My aunt said Rob was horrified and proclaimed that I should take all the time I needed to. I was afraid Rob was going to give my job away to someone else. I would have been devastated if my job was taken away from me because I really enjoyed working at the Record Den. It was an escape from what I would call a mundane existence at the time.

The owner, Rob Petrowski, was probably the best boss I ever had, even though I felt he should ease up on his use of weed. He was too damned paranoid, always worrying about the business going under. "It's this damned compact disc, man," he would bitch and moan to me. "Nobody's interested in vinyl anymore. These yuppies, they're only interested in white wine, coke and compact discs."

Now, when Rob was talking about coke, he wasn't talking about the soft drink. It was the white snow-like substance that people sniffed up their noses. Rob was a weed head, although he had done stronger drugs such as cocaine, acid and angel dust, but that drug history was at least 12 years ago. The "1988 Rob," pushing 40 years old, had become strictly a beer and weed guy. He had left the hard drugs behind.

The East Village was becoming gentrified before our eyes. More yuppies were moving in, and there were less artist types. You still had the NYU college crowd, and those kids were Rob's biggest clientele. Then you would have the usual assortment of burned-out hippies, white suburban kids from Jersey, punks with multi-colored hair or mohawks, heavy metal kids decked out in long hair and motorcycle jackets, or perhaps just record collectors in search of that lost LP that had been out of print before being released on compact disc.

I couldn't deny Rob's assessment that the neighborhood was changing. A couple of high-end clothing boutiques had opened up along 8th Street and a new trendy restaurant, called Le Bistro, was becoming the rage. I ate there just after it had opened a month earlier and was mortified by the prices. Ten dollars for a lousy hamburger? It was greasy and overcooked. I could go down to McDonald's and get a hamburger, fries and a drink for half that price.

Not everyone owned a CD player. CDs alone were $18 a pop, while records were priced at least $10. While the clarity of sound while playing a compact disc was quite crystalline, the CD was rather expensive. I knew of only one person who had a compact disc player at that time, an acquaintance of mine heavily into Madonna who played me one of her discs on his portable system. But collecting CDs was a very costly proposition and, besides, not a lot of records were available on compact disc then.

Before working at the Record Den, I was searching for a lost album by the Incredible Bongo Band that has a killer instrumental track on it called "Apache," and I didn't have to look very far, because Rob had it.

I started working for Rob the previous spring. My friend Brian Killian and I were checking out the record shops in Greenwich Village. At the time, I had a paper route I was tired of, and I was looking for a new job, but not a Toys R Us type of job. I wanted something unique. This seemed like the place.

Killian suggested that I ask the guy behind the counter if I could work there. The man was a graying long-haired hippie with a beard and glasses. He seemed genial enough, but I was a bit hesitant to ask.

"I don't know. I feel a little weird about this," I told Killian.

Killian, in his usual inimitable style, cut right through the bullshit. "Stop being such a pussy. You want a job, ask the guy."

"Excuse me," I asked timidly. "Are you hiring anyone?"

Killian gave me a "What the hell is wrong with you" look. A bad question to ask. "Be more assertive." But I had never asked for a job before. The job I did have, the paper route, was given to me by a neighbor's son before he went off to college.

The man's ears perked up. "Do you want to work here? I need someone on Saturdays. Are you up for it?"

"How much is the pay?" Killian asked. "And how many hours?"

"The pay is five dollars an hour, and you would work 10 hours on Saturday, from 10 in the morning to 8 at night."

I looked at Killian. Killian looked at me with a "Wake up, Stupid" kind of look. "Take the job. It's better than being a paper boy," he said simply.

"Yes," I affirmed. "I'm up for it."

"Cool," the owner said. "Can you start next Saturday?"

That query took me by surprise. I still had my paper route and would have to look for a replacement. But a week was more than enough time to find one. There was a neighborhood kid who was interested in my route, and she had been badgering me about whether I was ever quitting.

"Definitely," I said.

"Okay, I'll see you next week. Ten o'clock."

I was hired on the spot just like that and gave the route to the badgering neighborhood girl. And so I had been working at the Record Den for the past several months before my mugging, and I couldn't have imagined working anywhere else. The best thing about that job was I that I got paid to listen to music, and I discovered many different artists and genres I never would have found on the radio. I didn't always have the money to buy albums, and I could sample music without taking it home.

There weren't any downsides with the job per se. You may get a difficult and demanding customer now and then who would want a particular album for almost nothing, but as Rob stated, all prices were non-negotiable. And once in a while, you'd get a homeless person coming in begging for change. Rob didn't stand for that. He had compassion for the homeless, but he didn't wish to start a habit of giving out change indiscriminately and attracting a criminal element to the store.

It was usually Rob and myself on Saturdays at the shop. Sometimes I'd be alone for much of the day. My Saturdays were spent at the Record Den, while I would have Sundays free to study or do what I liked. Rob had the Sunday shift covered with Erika, a punkette a year older than me. I really didn't see much of her in those early days, but she seemed pleasant enough.

The atmosphere at the Record Den was relaxed, or was it the smoke emanating from Rob's joints that were making me mellow? I felt an inner peace there I never felt while I was in school. I often joked with Rob that perhaps I should quit school and become a lifer, working for him.

"No, no, you need your education, man," Rob would admonish me. But I loved working at the Record Den. It was an escape from my otherwise boring, mundane life, consisting of just studying and going to school, and the occasional hanging out with friends.

My ultimate ambition was to go to film school. Aunt Jane wanted me to go to a proper college and major in business, but I wasn't feeling any great affinity for the field.

Killian and Me

Brian Killian came over the weekend before the start of my final semester as a high school student. Our friendship went back 11 years, since the time I moved onto Staten Island. Killian was two years older, but that age difference never affected us. We had always been tight. Killian was studying at the Julliard school. He was an aspiring musician, and he had the look of the '80s metal head, with the long flowing light brown curly locks cascading past his shoulders. He was a pretty boy, which I often told him, much to his dismay. But it was all good-natured, caustic banter.

Killian worked in a guitar shop on 48th Street in the city. We Staten Islanders always refer to the borough of Manhattan as "the city." Staten Island is known as the burbs, because I guess it's so suburban compared with the rest of the city. And some say would say dull, but it's quieter, and before this mugging I would have said safer, but I had to revise that opinion.

The pretty boy was also a Staten Islander like me, living on the border of the Clifton/Rosebank section with his parents in a beautiful Victorian home on Townsend Avenue just up from the old Colonial Lanes on Bay Street. Killian was gigging with a punk rock band called High Octane. I couldn't tell you the significance of the name. Perhaps the band should have been titled High Methane, because they simply stank to high heaven. It was typical punk metal sludge, which was a style that did nothing for me. His band generated a ton of noise, totally amateurish and indecipherable. Killian is an adept guitarist, but he was wasting his time playing with those clowns. I told him as much and he would get offended, but he knew I was right on the money. In all fairness, my personal tastes were not in punk/metal but more toward '70s progressive music. There wasn't much rock and roll I was interested in, save for Genesis, Yes and Pink Floyd, where it sounded professional. The Beatles were my absolute favorite when it came to pop. Those guys were the masters, and still are after all these years.

I was glad for Killian's company, because I really needed it. This mugging had gotten me all depressed, and I needed some good cheer. Better yet, I needed a target to rag on. Ragging each other was our favorite sport, and we managed to take it very well as much as dishing it out to one another. We mostly shot the breeze over the TV blaring in the background, goofing on the quality of the programming. Cable had finally landed on Staten Island, and instead of just 10 channels of shit, there were now 60. But I was housebound and what else did I have to do?

The Name 'Roddy'

I'm the only Roddy I have ever known except for the "Planet of the Apes" actor Roddy McDowall and the ex-pro wrestler Roddy Piper. I always despised my first name. It was so different from every other name I was accustomed to at the time. Why not Michael or John? I didn't like standing out from the crowd, and that name brought me lots of abuse. It wasn't until Rowdy Roddy Piper burst onto the scene that I found I could have a little bit of pride in the name I have.

It was on a winter's day in January 1984 when I first laid eyes on the Rowdy One. I was watching cheapie NY TV station WOR, which televised WWF wrestling, and here's this guy wearing a blue dress shirt and a kilt being introduced by some nerdy looking WWF official. "Piper's Pit," a five-minute interview segment, was launched and the microphone was passed over to Piper himself. Piper started to butter up the official, then he started to lambaste him, calling his interview techniques stupid and alluding to him being an ass kisser, although not in those words. I found it hilarious, and it became a Saturday morning ritual for me to rush through my paper route and catch "Piper's Pit," which sometimes was superior to the matches themselves. "Piper's Pit" was caustic, hilarious and unpredictable. Roddy Piper, who was ordinary looking and not fearsome, turned out to be the whole show of wrestling for me, even over America's favorite, Hulk Hogan. Did I identify with Piper because of my Scottish heritage, or did I love the way he would verbally cut up people? I wished I had that ability back at age 14, but I had trouble speaking. I stammered, only answering questions when I had to and saying as little as possible. I only wish I had the ability to verbally spar back then. Perhaps I could have put a few of those thugs who used to make my life a living hell for me in their place. It was now fashionable for me to have the name Roddy. Some kids taunted me by calling me Roddy Piper, but I took that as a compliment. Piper was proud of his Scottish heritage and could back it all up.

From the stories I have heard about the man, he is a legitimate tough guy, leaving home as a teen, growing up on city streets and entering the pro wrestling world at the age of 17. I know pro wrestling is premeditated, but Piper was the real deal. Roddy Piper specialized in being a heel, antagonizing the good-guy wrestlers and the fans. He was the wrestler that fans loved to hate for two years in a row, until suddenly he transformed himself into a good guy, agitating the "heel wrestlers," winning fans and outdistancing Hulk Hogan in popularity. And at the height of his popularity, Piper retired from wrestling to pursue an acting career. When that occurred, my retirement from watching wrestling transpired. I was no longer interested.

The Beginnings

I was born in the Highbridge section of the South Bronx at the start of the 1970s. My father was a bartender, and he was killed in a blaze set by arsonists only two years after I was born, one of many fires set in the South Bronx at that time. Highbridge was the neighborhood I was raised in for almost seven years of my life. My mom worked as a nurse's assistant, supporting her and myself, having been left a widow. We lived in a building still populated by mostly Irish, despite the neighborhood around us being already overwhelmingly Hispanic. Highbridge had morphed into the South Bronx, one of the more infamous crime slums in America.

I wasn't really aware of the neighborhood being a trouble zone. I lived a sheltered life that consisted of homework, play and Saturday morning cartoons. When my mom wasn't home, I would stay with the Floreses, a Puerto Rican family. There was the husband and wife team of Miguel and Patricia and their daughter, Jasmine. Miguel was a maintenance man, and Patricia, like my mom, was a nurse's aide at Montefiore General Hospital.

Jasmine was three years older than myself. She was my closest friend during that period. We were always out on the street in front of the apartment house playing stickball with a bunch of neighborhood Hispanic kids. The other kids seemed to accept me, although I was always called "Blanco." Jasmine was the one who taught me how to hit a ball and field. Sometimes we would walk over to Macombs Dam Park, which was in the shadow of Yankee Stadium. If the weather was too cold outside, school afternoons after homework were spent watching the WABC 4:30 movie.

Jasmine was my coach and protector as well. She would often help me complete my homework if I was having problems; and since we both attended the same school, she often walked home with me.

One of the many memories I have of that neighborhood was of a youth street gang that called itself the Vandals. The members looked fearsome and intimidating with their floppy hats and cut-off denim and leather vests with a painting of the grim reaper on the back. I remember walking home with Jasmine one spring afternoon after school, and the Vandals were all hanging on a stoop. They saw us coming and decided to have a little fun at our expense. One guy jumped right in front of my face, snarling at me with a gleaming switchblade dangling near my nose. Another wagged his tongue at Jasmine. Jasmine simply steered me away from the gang, and we pushed our way through. The gang, happy with their brand of entertainment, gave one another high-fives.

"Those boys are bad news," Jasmine pointed out to me. "Don't ever go near them!"

What I would learn about those gangs years later is that they thought they were saving the neighborhood, chasing out junkies and pushers. However, chasing junkies and pushers was not a full-time occupation. They would turn their attention to the locals and terrorize them, often hitting the shop owners up for protection money. And many of them became involved in the drug trade when they saw how much money it could bring in. Some became addicts themselves. Others either were simply killed off in the gang wars or imprisoned. If some were lucky, they turned around their lives for the better.

Fire engines were a common sight in Highbridge. Not a day went by when you didn't hear those sirens. And then there was the smell of smoke in the air. You could also see it blackening the sky, as well as red orange flames dancing from the apartment windows into the sky. Those flames scared the hell out of me when I was a kid. It was almost as if they were evil spirits. I remember this one building across the street that arsonists set on fire. The flames were wildly dancing out of the windows , the air thick with smoke while the residents below, now made homeless, were clutching their loved ones and whatever belongings they managed to salvage. The firefighters rolled up in their engines, doing their best to train their hoses to drown out the fires, but it was futile. The next day, the building would be a shell of its former self, and that smoke smell never seemed to go away.

I often wondered why I would see the Floreses more often than my own mom. The family would tell me, "Your mom is sick, but she is getting better, and she will be home soon enough." It turned out my mom was not faring well at all. She was dying of leukemia during that spring of 1977. At one time, my mom was light-brown-haired and healthy looking, but now she resembled a living corpse, her hair all gone due to chemotherapy and looking twenty years older than her 40 years. But she never complained, and promised that she would be home soon.

If the woman was tough in facing down her illness, an incident the previous winter in our building shook her up. Our neighbor across the hallway, an elderly woman named Mrs. Finnigan, was beaten to death when her apartment was broken into. No one was sure whether it was junkies or the sick Vandals. All of the residents clammed up, for fear of retaliation by whoever it was. Nevertheless, I can never forget the sight of the EMTs carrying out a battered and bloodied Mrs. Finnigan on a stretcher, an oxygen mask placed over her.

My mom cried when they brought Mrs. Finnigan out to the ambulance. "My God, we have to move, we have to move," she said. "There is no way we can stay here, there is no way. We should have moved after your father died, but we couldn't afford to. But now we have no choice."

There were plans for us to move to Staten Island after my first-grade year was up. But my mom never made it to the finish line. She died two weeks earlier.

I remember seeing my mom just days before her death. There was no doubt she was dying, but she positively glowed when she saw me. "You're growing up fast. I'm missing all of this. But I'm not planning to miss any more of this. I'll be home soon, and we'll move out of that horrible place. It will be much better on Staten Island."

Her spirit was willing, but her weakened body was just unwilling to continue the brutal fight against the cancer. I remember during one of those last days of school, Jasmine and I came home to find her parents crying. Elena Flores took my face by her hands and said to me, "Roddy, I'm so sorry, but your mother died today. I'm so sorry, baby, I'm so sorry." She gave me a tight hug.

I was not yet 7 and I never understood death. I only started to have religious instruction that year. But all these terms of "God," "heaven" and "hell" seemed very strange for a child. "Where is Mom, and why can't I see her again?" I cried myself to sleep that night in the spare bed next to Jasmine's. Jasmine sensed what was going on, came over to my bed and cradled me.

What I did know about death was that my mom wasn't coming back, and that was a bad experience for any young kid.

After the school year was up, my Aunt Jane and Uncle Harry were taking custody of me. I was not thrilled with the news, because I really wanted to stay with the Floreses. I remember Mr. Flores telling me, "Roddy, I want you to stay, Mrs. Flores wants you to stay and Jasmine wants you to stay, but you can't. You have to go live with your aunt and uncle. Your mom wanted that if she died. They are your godparents."

"No!" I screamed in anger. "I don't want to go, I won't go!" But I had no choice in the matter.

The Floreses themselves took me to Staten Island, where my Uncle Harry and Aunt Jane lived on a hilly residential street named St. John's Avenue in Rosebank. Even Jasmine said, "Oh, I want to live here. This is so nice. Mom, Dad, do we really have to go back to the Bronx?"

All of the Floreses gave me a hug before they left. Jasmine was the one who was breaking up the most. "Please write to me, Roddy," she said. "I'll miss you."

My last memory of the Flores family was of their station wagon departing for the Bronx and Jasmine in the back seat, crying and waving. I never did write Jasmine. In my young mind, she reminded me of Mom, and I just wanted to forget.

Staten Island Life

Life on Staten Island was definitely quieter than in the Bronx. I was able to get outside more. It was on Staten Island that I first learned to ride a bike, with my Uncle Harry holding it from the tail end. Even though our house had a back yard, our true back yard was the nearby thirty-square-acre Von Briesen Park, which overlooked New York with a view of New York Harbor. To the far left, you had commanding views of the industry of Port Elizabeth/ Newark, New Jersey and the skyline of Manhattan with the Twin Towers standing tall; in the center, the neighborhood of Bay Ridge, Brooklyn; and to the far east, Coney Island, with the Parachute Jump needle sticking out.

I loved playing in this park, running down the small steep hills, letting the wind carrying me. How can I forget the fall leaves crunching beneath my sneakers, then sliding down the hills on a sled during wintertime, or the gentle breezes of spring with the trees and flowers blooming?

There was a baseball little league field on Summer Street just a few blocks from the park. Uncle Harry signed me up, but I was not a ballplayer: I couldn't hit or field. I could pitch decently, but what was the point if I couldn't do the other fundamentals of baseball? Even if you pitch, you still have to field your position. I still enjoyed watching baseball on TV, especially the Philadelphia Phillies. And how does a Bronx boy become a fan of the Philadelphia Phillies? It must have been the maroon pinstriped uniforms. I found them so damned attractive, even over the Bronx Bombers' pinstripes.

That was the era of Mike Schmidt, Tug McGraw, Pete rose, Lefty Steve Carlton, Greg Luzinski, Garry Maddox and Larry Bowa. Those guys made a phenomenal team. I remember the trips Uncle Harry and I would take to Veterans Stadium in South Philly. Uncle Harry would order each of us soft pretzels, Philly cheese-steaks and Cokes. The noise inside "the Vet" was astounding and deafening. Phillies fans are quite intense and vocal. If a player hits a homerun, the crowd will cheer so vociferously, that the noise will force that player out of the dugout for a curtain call. And fans can boo their own players if they feel they are not giving a good effort. Phillies fans like players who wear their emotions on their sleeves, not nonchalant lackadaisical players. With opposing players, they are worse. They have actually caused opposing pitchers to lose control of what they are doing and have emotional breakdowns on the mound.

My favorite was Mike Schmidt. "Schmitty" is the greatest third baseman of all time. The homers he hit were mile-high and -long. And his fielding was impeccable. I have seen the man make plays barehanded! I have tried playing third base, and I almost had my head taken off by line drives. How did he make it look so damned easy, and on Astroturf too? But the fans would boo him if he struck out, yet the man always gave his all. I couldn't understand the Phillies fans' way of thinking. Here you had one of the greatest players of all time, yet you are booing him for an off day? How many other teams would have loved to have this guy playing third base?

I was ecstatic when the Phillies won it all in 1980. Uncle Harry actually took me down to Philadelphia, and there we were, among the throngs of people lining up on Broad Street. My God, I had never seen so many people in my life. And then there the flatbed trucks of the various players rolling by. I can't forget Tug McGraw holding up a newspaper with the headline "We Win!" It was such an awesome spectacle. Aunt Jane was not happy with Uncle Harry for letting me miss a school day, but it was one of those once-in-a-lifetime moments you can never forget. Uncle Harry was more of a Yanks fan, but he was willing to bend over backward to accommodate my love of the Phillies.

I was pretty much a loner as a kid attending local public school. Every year, there seemed to be an antagonist wanting to make my life miserable. Intermediate school was where my troubles would worsen. The first year wasn't so bad. I was placed in the SPE class, a program for gifted or smart kids, but the problem was that I wasn't too bright. The other kids sensed I wasn't in their league, and while they were never physically abusive to me, they weren't afraid to be verbally abusive, often putting me down for not being intelligent. But my biggest problem was a mathematics teacher who seemed to get off on embarrassing me in front of the class. Mr. Parsino was a toupee-wearing, mustachioed prick who loved nothing more than to yell at kids who had trouble understanding algebra. I was one of his prized targets. Sad to say, I was never a good math student. But when a kid is having difficulty with the work, you don't ridicule him for his lack of understanding; you try to help him. I may not know much about teaching, but that is uncalled-for behavior. My confidence was shattered in his class. I can't tell you how many times I studied my brains out for his tests, but my efforts were never good enough to pass. For all that abuse he gave me, I should have asked Parsino why he wore that ridiculous rug on his head. It looked like road kill. Could you suspend a kid for asking that?

In the eighth grade, I was not only verbally abused but physically abused as well. I was a magnet for punks who got their kicks from punching and smacking me around. And the saddest, most disgraceful part about this mess was that I didn't do a single thing to defend myself. I just lay down for the bastards. The smacks against the head, the kicks in the rear end, the claps against the ears, or being tossed into a thorn bush on the side of the school where I came out with my face all scratched up. I did absolutely nothing, and if I at least tried to fight back, perhaps I would have won some respect from the punks, where they wouldn't have tried to fuck with me.

The worst thing about that year was a betrayal by a "buddy" of mine, Robert Hewlett. I met him at the tail end of the seventh grade during gym class, and he seemed to be a nice enough kid. We had the same interests in history and *Star Wars* science fiction. I used to talk baseball a lot, and I know he wasn't interested, but everyone is different.

The friendship went downhill during the eighth grade. Robert was a very moody kid. One minute, he was happiness and light; the next minute, he could really be a sneaky bastard. He was given to playing practical jokes; in other words, stuffing cafeteria hamburgers in my book bag or smearing peanut butter on my clothes. Practical jokes are harmless fun, but this was mean-spirited stuff.

I had trouble with the school punks because I didn't have the guts or courage to stand up for myself. I had no self-respect or self-confidence, and when you have neither, you're quite vulnerable. Robert definitely took advantage of that. He was the one person I felt I could confide in. At one point, I told him that if only I had the courage, I would defend myself better and I would get revenge. He gave this information to Tony Mecari, one of the thugs who was after my ass for whatever sick reason those bastards got off on. Mecari then threatened to kill me if I even thought about seeking revenge. Robert denied telling him, but who the hell did?

Tony Mecari was a vicious son of a bitch, no doubt about it, although at least he was honest and upfront. He certainly was no friend, so I knew what to expect from him. I had expected more from Robert since he was a friend I had put a lot of trust in.

I'm not sure what has happened to Robert, because I lost contact with him and I needed to keep my distance. Robert would call up my house phone number and play a game of tapping a button, where all you would hear was a beep but no voice. It took me a while to figure out who it was. Uncle Harry and Aunt Jane were irritated by this prank to say the least, and when my Uncle Harry got upset about it, I knew there was a serious problem. That's because it took quite a lot for that man to get mad. Robert gave himself away when we were arguing over the phone and he decided to tap on some buttons. The way the buttons sounded when he tapped down on them was the tipoff.

The worst of it was near the end of that semester. We had gym class out in the schoolyard. For whatever reason, a bunch of punks decided to grab me and tie me up against the fence, placing a loose branch between the belt buckles of my pants and slipping it through the fence holes. Then the whole bunch of them proceeded to smack the shit out of me. Robert was one of them.

I don't know what happened to Robert after intermediate school. The same with Mecari. I do realize now that the two of them had some issues back then, and I can only wish them well.

I changed after intermediate school. I became much more introverted and quieter than usual, refusing to say anything to anyone unless it was to friends I already knew. My demeanor became sour, and I wouldn't laugh so easily for another four years. I made a solemn promise to myself that no one would ever physically abuse me again.

The physical abuse wouldn't happen again because I would fight at the drop of a hat; however, the verbal abuse never stopped. I was horrible at verbal confrontation. I didn't have the quick-thinking capability required to fight back in a verbal fashion. The verbal abuse finally relented after freshman year of high school, but I became a recluse and withdrew into myself.

I didn't have a whole lot of friends in school. The most amount of "hanging out" I ever did was with Killian. Other than that, I would just stay at home. Contact with the opposite sex? Oh, there was a conversation or two, but nothing serious.

The one incident that truly devastated me was the loss of my Uncle Harry in the spring of '87. He was only 53 years old. Aunt Jane and I never expected it. The man looked healthy and always ready with a smile. I came home that terrible spring afternoon to find Aunt Jane crying while trying to slice cucumbers over the kitchen table. Aunt Jane is a tough woman, and I'd never seen her so distraught like I did that day. When she announced that Uncle Harry had passed away, I was shocked. We did not know of any health problems with him. The bus driver for the MTA of NYC had gone about his daily routine of driving his route, but he had left work early that day, complaining of chest pains. While at the doctor's office, Uncle Harry suffered a massive heart attack, and he was rushed to the hospital. But by the time he reached the ER, he was pronounced dead.

I was angry at Aunt Jane for not contacting me at school. This had happened in the morning hours, so why couldn't she have pulled me out of class that day?

"For God sakes, lad, he is dead!" Aunt Jane cried. "I didn't even get a chance to say goodbye to him meself."

Just like that, the man who had been a father figure to me for the past 10 years was dead. I remember him over the course of those high school years trying his best to find out what was going on in my head. Why was I struggling in school? Why did I seem no longer chipper? I had told him I had always been getting a hard time from other kids, but that I was getting a good handle on it. Uncle Harry suggested I tell a school official if I was having a problem with anyone before fighting. I would rather not have done that, because if other kids heard, I would have been called a tattletale, and who knew how many more beatings I would have to take. Looking back, I was upset with myself about not sharing with him. I was too ashamed to talk to Uncle Harry about my problems. My conduct had been disgraceful, because here was a man who had tried to help, and I just pushed him away. In my stupid mind, he was this corny middle-aged guy driving a bus, but he was a lot wiser than most people I knew.

He worked hard to provide for his wife and his nephew. My biggest thrill with him was always watching the latest movies on videotape, talking baseball and those occasional trips to the Vet. Those conversations and trips would be no more, and I had a lot of guilt to deal with. It's sad. He had asked me a week earlier if I would be interested in seeing the Phillies at Shea Stadium. I told him no, and when I said this, he looked confused and a bit hurt. Maybe he thought his nephew felt himself "too cool" to hang out with his uncle anymore. But part of it was that the Phillies were no longer a good team, falling into the second division. Most of the stars had retired; and if there were any left, they were aging. And the minor league system of the Phillies wasn't coming up with any replaceable talent. But the "too cool" part was true too — who am I kidding? It seemed rather boring and old hat to go to a ball game with your uncle. But if I had just accepted, maybe the man would still be alive. Did he die because of a broken heart, broken because his nephew wouldn't confide in him anymore and wouldn't take the time to attend a lousy ball game with him? He probably did, and I'll never forgive myself for that.

Baby Steps

It was hard stepping outside the door my first day back at school after the attack. I don't think I had been outside since I came home from the hospital. My left wrist was wrapped in an ace bandage; and although the swelling and bruises had lessened on my face, I still looked worse for the wear. The taped ribs were healing slowly but surely. But it felt as if my upper torso had been crushed. I never wore a scarf for anything, but I had to wear one that day. The cold air slashed through me like a knife, and it was hard breathing with ribs that weren't quite healed. The No. 78 bus for Hylan Boulevard seemed to be taking longer than usual. When it came, I went on board, and the looks from the crowd, mostly students, were asking, "What in the hell happened to you?" That was the kind of look I would be receiving all day. Who can forget the questions: "What happened to you?" "Who beat you up?"

I can't tell you how many times that day I heard that line of interrogation over and over. I wanted to answer, "I slipped and fell while skateboarding," but idiotic me, honest Roddy, had to explain the truth. When girls would ask me, they would go, "Awwww." It was nice to have their sympathy, but at the same token, I was sufficiently annoyed. In order to get respect, did I almost have to pay with my life?

The best part of that first day was when it was confirmed that Brenda Moriarty was my teacher for the creative writing class. There she was, the tall, red-headed, spiky-haired woman with the sparkling blue eyes and smile. She shot me a wave when she noticed me sitting in the back corner of the room next to the window. I always tried to situate myself in that seat, because I wanted to isolate myself from the crowd.

Brenda introduced herself to the class, which mostly consisted of females — the brainiac type, although you had a few airheads in there with the big hair. But that's a generalization, because not all big-haired girls were bubble-headed. It was the style of the times: the bigger the hair, the better. The class numbered 27. I was one of five boys. There wasn't going to be any jocks in the class; they had no interest, unless it was to leer at Brenda Moriarty. Since this was her first year at the school, not too many kids would have known about her, but then again, how could you not notice the prettiest teacher in the entire school?

Writing was never thought as a pursuit for young teenage males. Living as a male teenager on Staten Island, you often got the sense of what was manly and what was not. I couldn't very well tote around a notebook along Staten Island unless I wanted to encounter serious beatings from the other kids. So I outwardly followed my love of baseball, which was not frowned upon. Since I was Phillies fan in hostile territory, it wouldn't have been wise to announce my allegiance to the other kids, who mostly followed the New York Mets, the Phillies' main division rival.

Brenda was very cordial yet straightforward. "This class is an elective, which means all of you want to be here. And you know by the title of the course that you will all be writing. And I mean lots of writing," she said. "The only thing I require from each and every one of you is to complete the assignments. Yes, you will work hard in this class, and it's not an easy elective. But you will have a lot of fun. You're going to enjoy this class.

"What we are going to be doing today is writing about ourselves. "Who am I?" will be the topic. You will have 15 minutes to complete this. You can start now."

The class fell silent and put pens to paper with their eyes glued to their desks. I tapped my pen against my cheek and wondered what in the hell I could write about. She must have sensed I was having trouble, because her voice called out: "If you are having trouble, just write, don't think. Go with the flow."

Of course. That works, I realized; and this is what I came up with:

"Who am I? I'm just a raggedy senior in Normand High School trying to find his way in life. Everyone around me feels that I should have a clear definition of what I should be doing with myself after high school. I'm just a kid, for crying out loud! I don't have a set pattern on life and I really don't know what I should be doing with myself once high school is all over. Should everyone at age 17 or 18 have a clear path and walk along it? There are a few hedges and trees in my way that need to be chopped down before I can walk along that path, but I don't know how I can. I'm just a scrub who has been fortunate to reach his senior year in high school and hopefully graduate in five months. What are my plans? I don't know yet. I know I'll probably work after school. As far as college goes, I don't know if I'm interested. I'm not bright enough for high school, so what on earth makes me think I'll do well in college?

"I don't know who I am. I'm just a kid sitting in a corner of a classroom who has been told by others he will soon be an adult and that he must be responsible. Who knows what or where I will be tomorrow. For all I know, I could get struck by lightning or a car wreck today. God knows, I have cheated death after being mugged over a week ago.

"But I don't think I'm Morris the Cat, where I'll have Nine Lives. I'll just take it day by day. It's never good to make dreams or plans, because they don't always work out."

The teacher had started off with the students on the other side of the room, and by the time the class ended, they weren't even close to getting around to me. And as fate would have it, I wasn't struck by a car or lightning that afternoon after school.

But I was up at bat the following day to read my essay. I was the "grand finale." The class chuckled at my essay, especially the bit where I mused about getting struck by a car or lightning.

"That was fantastic," Brenda enthused. "I loved the sarcastic humor of it all. But you're way too pessimistic. You'll be fine."

Now, I don't know why in the hell this came out of my mouth, but it did. Usually, I was very close-mouthed in class, but not this day: "Maybe you should write about yourself. We're going to be stuck with you for the next five months, so we should know who we are dealing with."

A slight "Ooohhh" reverberated throughout the class. I wasn't trying to be a smartass, although it did sound like I was doing a good impersonation of one. Brenda appeared amused by the whole deal.

"Oh, okay," she responded. "Just give me seven minutes; that's all I need."

It took her five minutes to write what she had to say:

"Who am I? My name is Brenda Moriarty, and I have been a high school English teacher for close to seven years. I love teaching on the high school level, and I have no problem dealing with teenagers. They say teenagers are the most difficult group of people to teach. I've had my share of disciplinary problems, but I've weathered them. Teenagers are very misunderstood, and no one else should ever condemn a whole group since some are troubled. There are many exemplary kids out there who are quite responsible and even better than some adults. To know teenagers is to love them.

"While I'm not teaching, I'm studying for a master's degree. I want to earn a Ph.D., where I can teach on the college level. I'm not bored with high school teaching, yet there could be a time in the future where this job no longer exhilarates me as it does now. There's also the money factor, which is an added incentive.

"I was once married, but I've been divorced for three years. If the right man comes along, I would definitely get married again, but as for now, my career is my primary focus."

After Brenda was finished, she looked up at me and asked with a smile, "Are you satisfied?"

I was surprised she took up my challenge. If I were her, I would have been pissed off at me for trying to make her look foolish in front of the entire class.

"Oh, I'm satisfied, now," I said. "At least I know who we are dealing with. For all we know, you could have been a mutant from outer space."

The class cracked up on that comment. Even Brenda was laughing. "He's cute, isn't he?" she remarked to the class. "The last time I checked, I'm a human being," Brenda affirmed, tongue firmly in cheek. "No little monsters are popping out of my stomach. You remember *Alien*?"

"That's good," I answered back. "If I saw a sight like that in real life, I would have run so fast out of here."

"I'm so glad you are happy, because from now on, whenever the class has an assignment to read, you will go first."

The class "Oohed" again. "Shut up!" my mind screamed.

"That's right, sweetie," she said, smiling at me devilishly. "I'm a witch with a capital 'B,' and I always get even."

There was more laughter from the class. This was entertainment unwittingly supplied by my challenge and taken up by the English teacher. I did show her up in front of the classroom, so I got my just deserts. Fair enough, but I guess it could have been worse. I could have gotten a stern lecture about how I was the student, and that it was my responsibility, not the teacher's, to perform the assignment.

Would it have done any good to apologize to Brenda after the class was over? In my mind, whatever was done was done, and I immediately exited the class when the bell sounded.

Hard-Assed Teachers

It would turn out that Brenda would become an ally and a staunch supporter of mine during this last semester of high school. I would have problems with several of the other teachers.

One of the classes I had opted to take was an art class in order to fulfill my elective requirements. The teacher was Mr. Crano, an older man who resembled one of those vaudeville villains with the pencil-thin mustache, which he had, along with the slicked-back hair. I figured Crano to be in his early 60s, which meant he had one foot out the door, and his attitude displayed that. He probably couldn't wait to retire. All Crano did that first day was lace into the students, deeming us "useless" and reprimanding us for our selfishness. "You all should be grateful for the education you are getting instead of being lazy and spoiled."

Crano couldn't help but notice that some of us were seniors, and we received the lecture that we had better pay attention and do well in his class. If we didn't, it would not be his fault if we were confused by the lessons. And if we failed, we wouldn't be able to graduate, and that would not be his problem, but ours. Someone should have reminded the man that the class was an elective, not a requirement for graduation. Right away I sensed that he would be trouble. That first day was spent lecturing the class, so no classroom work was assigned.

We dived into the lessons the second day by attempting to draw three-dimensional lettering. Now, I am no artist, but I wanted to take the course thinking it would be fun. Crano is definitely a talented artist. He was designing that letter work as if it was second nature. I had trouble following along.

Crano took one look at my outline of measuring and was less than enthralled with my handiwork.

"Don't you know how to measure? What the hell is the matter with you? This is garbage, utter crap!" He took my "attempted art" and, in a dramatic display, crumpled it in his hands and tossed it

into the waste paper basket. The frustrated artist and burned-out
teacher handed me a new sheet. "If you can't follow these meas-
urements," he told me, "I don't know what in the hell I can do for
you. And what the hell happened to you that you're all beat up like
this?"

"I was mugged, sir."

"What a world! It gets worse and worse!"

At least the guy could have said, 'Sorry,' but I gathered I was
lucky to get that much out of him.

Brenda Moriarty's class was right after Crano's, and hers was
the last class of the day. Her class was light and breezy in contrast
to Crano's, with none of the tension that he brought to the table.

Then again, you are talking about two different personali-
ties. One was uptight, burned-out and controlling; the other
was gracious, patient and good-natured. On the third day of
classes, there was no writing done. Instead there was an in-depth
examination of a short story in which two neighbors, a man and
woman, are cheating with each other on their spouses. At the
end, the narrator has to end the affair because the spouses are
getting suspicious.

I was less than impressed with the story, and I voiced my
opinion.

"These people should be shot," I blurted out. "They have the
morals of sewer rats."

The class, including Brenda, chuckled at that statement. "I definitely agree with you," Brenda said. "I'm not impressed with the
story myself, but I wanted to give all of you the idea that you can
create stories about any subject matter, no matter how misguided
they are."

After the class, Brenda asked me how I was coming along.

"I'm getting better," I answered. "It's taking me some time."

"It will. You were hurt very badly. How are you liking the class?"

"It's early to tell yet. I'm not sure."

Brenda gave me a quizzical look. "What are you not sure about?"

I shook my head in uncertainty. "I don't think I'm going to do
well in this class. I don't have the writing ability."

"Oh, yes, you do," Brenda insisted. "That first essay about yourself was well written with a lot of sardonic humor. You're just lacking confidence in yourself. I hope you are not thinking of dropping out of this class?"

That was the furthest idea from my mind. I wanted to drop out of Crano's class, but that was a totally different matter.

"No, I don't want to," I confirmed, "but I feel I won't be able to live up to your standards."

Brenda was puzzled. "I'm not following you."

I sighed. "I know I deserved a penalty for showing you up the other day, but I don't think it's a good idea to have me lead off. Are you going to be measuring me against the other students?"

"You worry too much. I wasn't mad about yesterday. I thought it was cute, although I was surprised you would come out with that. I can see you're shy by sitting in that corner, but I have a feeling you want to break out of that shell in this class. That's great. But do me a favor. Please don't leave this class. I'll be very sad if you do. You'll have a lot of fun here, and I know you are going to be just fine."

How could I not stay in the class with all that confidence behind me?

Acquaintances and Friends

"Those people are animals," my friend John Corsi ranted in Italian class after I had told him of the mugging. I couldn't dispute that apt description. The attack was so brutal and swift, it was a wonder I had survived it.

I grew up as a little boy in the South Bronx, but I was packed away from that tough neighborhood when I was only 7, and for 11 years before the mugging, I had been reared in suburban-styled Staten Island. Growing up in a soft world could never have prepared me for that beating. And I was tired of all of the questions about what had happened. I should have answered, "I slipped and fell down the stairs at home." It would have been a lot easier to explain it all away. Perhaps I would have been labeled a klutz, but for the ones who would even gave a shit, it would have left them satisfied.

Corsi was genuine. He was really witty about the whole ordeal, claiming it was the drugs that were the root cause of all this, the crack cocaine epidemic. You would never, ever think that such an experience would happen to you. There are so many stories in the newspapers about violent crime, but it all seems fictitious until you're involved directly or even indirectly. My first exposure to violent crime was witnessing the paramedics carrying Mrs. Finnigan out on a stretcher from our Bronx tenement building 11 years ago. I didn't witness her attack, but I certainly experienced it 11 years later for myself.

John Aquino, my best friend during lunch period, was astonished. He looked up long enough from drooling over his 8-by-10 Madonna photo to talk to me about the crime. This was odd behavior for him, because his eyes were constantly glued to that photo. I never saw the bastard ever eat a morsel while in the cafeteria. It was as if his appetite was sated by the glossy Madonna photo in his loose-leaf notebook.

He asked me the question John Corsi had asked me: "Why the hell did you go over to the St. George Library?" Very simply, it was the best library on Staten Island. But what I wasn't going to tell them was that I was trying to research my family. I never knew my father, and I barely knew my mother. It's only natural for an orphan to want to know more about his parents.

I attended Normand High School, and my existence there had been relatively peaceful.

The freshman year was the hardest since I was mostly verbally abused, but there were never any physical confrontations. The high school I was originally slated to attend was Curtis, located not too far from where I was mugged in St. George. My aunt and uncle persuaded me to attend Normand because Curtis had a reputation for violence. There were often reports of racial conflict, guns and knives. Even the blacks attending Normand were from the North Shore area of Staten Island, the more multiethnic side of the borough, and even their parents didn't want any part of Curtis. But I wonder if those kids ever felt ill at ease since Normand at the time was 80 percent white. There was racial conflict, but it was kept to a minimum. The one incident that stood out for me was a verbal slugfest between a guidettte and a black male. Apparently, they got into it, but I don't remember how. The white girl used the "n-word," and the black kid retorted with the word "slut." I remember one of the guidance counselors coming to my homeroom class and warning us about the harmful use of these words.

I was mostly isolated from these events. All I did was go to school, put in my time at my classes, finish up, get on the bus and go home.

This was a situation that would change for me greatly in this last semester.

The First Antagonist

It was only a week into the new semester when some little snot-nosed freshman punk shit named Robbie started to break my balls. He happened to share the same lunch period as me. I would have thought at this stage in the game that I would be through with these maggots, but no such luck. This little bastard came over to my table, saw my bruises, cuts and scrapes, and asked me what had happened. By this point, I was very well sick and tired of that question, but not to be rude, I simply answered, "An accident."

It wasn't enough for the parasite. He must have been about 5-foot-5. I stood at 5-foot-9, but he probably figured I was an easy mark. "Listen, faggot," the maggot said. "Tell me what happened, or I'll give you a beating just like that one you got. You didn't have an accident. You were mugged. Why are you fuckin' lying to me?"

Robbie's outburst definitely got the attention of my lunch table acquaintances, Joe Castigelli, Freddy McMahon and Aquino. Castigelli and McMahon stopped eating; Aquino stopped salivating over Madonna.

"Listen," I told Robbie. "Why don't you go back to your table and beat your meat? Leave me the fuck alone!" That comment cracked up our table. Robbie grew red in the face, glared at me and stated like all buffoons when their honor has been insulted: "You're dead, asshole. You're dead." I simply gave him the wave off. Robbie returned to his table, stewing over my wisecrack.

"That was a good one," commented McMahon.

"I'm sick and tired of this shit," I blurted out. "I don't need to be harassed."

If I thought that this was the end of the bullshit, I was sadly mistaken. On my way to the next class, who should accost me in the hallways but Robbie.

"Hey, faggot ass, I'm talking to you! Where the fuck ya think ya going?"

Before the mugging, I would have simply ignored the taunts and walked away, but my threshold for taking shit at that juncture was nil. My left wrist was still sprained, but this didn't stop me from approaching my tormentor. I immediately grasped his neck in a choke hold, backing him up against the wall. The parasite tried to flail at me with his fists, but to no avail. I followed up with a knee smash against his chest, which knocked the wind out of my tormentor and caused him to slump to the ground.

"Listen," I said to the breathless parasite that was on the ground, holding his chest in as he tried his best to gasp for some air. "Do not fuck around. I'll kill you. It's as simple as that!" I left the punk slumped against the wall and gasping for air. There were classes to attend. A few kids who witnessed this scene "Ooohed" at the site. They were assholes too, since they got off on that.

Violence was something I never got off on, but it was a necessary evil when dealing with dolts such as Robbie. If you don't show your fists, you're labeled a wimp and the abuse becomes unrelenting. It is absolutely extraordinary what a knee smash to the chest will accomplish. Robbie came over to my table the next day and offered to shake my hand.

"I never expected that," he enthused. "You are tough, even if you don't look it."

I shook his hand reluctantly, but I had no desire to associate with a scumbag such as this. "Just keep your ass to your table, and don't fuckin' bother me again. You remember what I said yesterday."

"No, no, we're cool, we're friends," he stated emphatically. He looked at me, trying to reassure me with his head nodding up and down while heading back to his seat.

Respect at Last

I wouldn't call what I gave Robbie a beating. It was a choke-hold and a knee smash to his midsection. But word got around the school about the altercation. Naturally, in a gossip hen house like high school, I was asked about this matter by numerous kids: "I heard you beat up a kid." All I did was grab him in a chokehold and give him a knee smash to the chest area. The "fight" lasted less than a minute.

Even Brenda Moriarty heard the rumors. "I heard you got into a fight yesterday," she remarked as she approached me after the writing class.

I sighed heavily. "It wasn't a fight. I gave the kid a knee smash to his chest. He was bothering me, so I decided to end it. Are you going to lecture me about how I should behave? I'm tired of taking shit from people."

My reaction took Brenda aback. "Don't get so defensive. Relax," she coaxed. "I'm on your side. I was your age once, and I had similar problems back then. There was this girl I knew back in my sophomore year. A real nasty, miserable person. She didn't like me for whatever screwed-up reason. At first it was verbal taunting, and then it led to her throwing rocks at me when I was walking home. I got so tired of her nonsense, I jumped on top of her and beat the living daylights out of her. The verbal taunting and the rock throwing came to a dead stop. So, no, Roddy, I don't blame you. I sense the kind of person you are, and I know you didn't start that fight. Boys in this age group can be little bastards, and girls can be little bitches. Sometimes a few kicks, smacks and punches are the only language they understand."

I was taken aback. "I'm surprised you would say that."

"Don't be," Brenda said. "I know you're a quiet kid who often stays to himself, am I right?"

I nodded.

"And quiet kids often attract an undesirable element, which are bullies. I know; I was a quiet kid myself back then. Other kids take your being quiet as a sign of weakness. You did what you had to do."

I was touched by Brenda's compassion. "Thanks for under-standing," I said.

Brenda rubbed me on the shoulder. "Anytime you need anyone to talk to, or a shoulder to cry on, just let me know, okay? I'll always have your back, hon."

I never had a teacher unequivocally in support of me, and it felt good to have that for a change. It was rather late in the game to have this support, but to use an old cliché, which was one that I used often when teachers would admonish me for my tardiness, "Better late than never."

The Prodigal Son Returns to Work

I absolutely couldn't wait to go back to the Record Den. But my aunt wasn't so enthralled with my imminent return. There was a major argument that week between my aunt and myself over my preferred workplace.

"It's too soon. Ye should rest, and that Manhattan is dangerous. Are ye looking to get yer noggin kicked in again?"

"I can't be afraid of going out, Aunt Jane," I protested. I have to live my life."

"Why don't ye get a job on the Island? Why not try Toys R Us, or Starlite Home Center on Forest Avenue?"

I tasted those ideas unhappily. I had no interest in toys, not since I was 10. And working at a hardware store seemed boring. But the extra income during the week wouldn't be such a bad thing. I weighed that option in my mind, and I knew for certain that Aunt Jane would force me to give up the record shop job if I did take one of those ghastly duties.

"No way, Aunt Jane. I'm not making myself miserable. I have a home in that job and I'm not giving it up."

"That job is yer home? Ye can't stay there forever. Wouldn't it be easier to stay closer to home?"

"Don't you understand I love working there? That place is my home away from home on a Saturday, and I get along with the people there." I could have also added that listening to music was an important part of my life. I loved the old, musty atmosphere of the place, the handling of the rare, mint-condition records, or perhaps a nicked and scratched record in a beat-up album sleeve. There was also the thrill of discovery when playing an unheard album that turned out to be fantastic. Yes, sometimes there would be difficult customers; but all in all, I loved the place and I couldn't imagine working anywhere else.

My aunt wasn't letting the discussion go. "That record store is no place to make a living, son. It's hard going. Is that all ye want to do with your life?"

I was starting to lose patience with my aunt. "No, I don't want to work there the rest of my life, but as long as I'm in high school, I'm working there."

"I hope yer not doing any drugs, young man," Aunt Jane warned me. "Those 'Manhattan artist types' are very weird. I wonder if they are missing parts of their brains."

"I don't touch that garbage, Aunt Jane." And it was the truth. But I certainly wasn't going to volunteer info about Rob's smoking joints in the back room. I inhaled plenty of those fumes while working in the shop, and those fumes no doubt accounted for the giddy moods I had during those days. But technically, I had never held a joint in my hands. If Aunt Jane were to find out about Rob's antics, she would go ballistic and forbid me from working there.

Despite Aunt Jane's misgivings, I went back to work, although I must own up that I was a bit nervous while traveling alone into the city. I found myself constantly looking over my shoulder. But I wasn't about to make this admission to my aunt.

When I arrived at the store, I was given a hero's welcome by two people: Rob Petrowski, the owner of the shop, and Erika Nielsen, the punkette who was usually the Sunday clerk but had been filling in on Saturdays in my stead. Both gave me hugs.

"I was so worried about you," said Erika. "I couldn't believe what had happened. How are you feeling?"

"It's taking time. I'm sore all over."

"Your face took a beating," Rob noticed, stating the obvious.

"I was kicked around like a football, Rob. What did you expect?"

"Did they catch the dudes who did this?" Rob inquired further.

"No, I haven't been unable to identify them. It happened so fast. The police couldn't believe I never saw them, but I had my eyes closed. All I heard above me was 'Get his fuckin' wallet, get his fuckin' wallet!'"

"What a bunch of bastards!" exclaimed Erika. "It's not the sort of thing you would expect to happen on Staten Island."

People who resided in the other boroughs of New York City have it in their heads that Staten Island is the last rural outpost. That may have been true at one time, but in the twenty-four years since the Verazzano Bridge was completed, the Island had changed dramatically. I had been a resident of the Island only for the past 11 years before these recent events, but I could tell you traffic had picked up tremendously. Bay Street and Hylan Boulevard, two main thoroughfares that were close to my home, were at times clogged with cars during the a.m. and p.m. rush hours. The Staten Island Expressway heading toward the Verrazano Bridge could be jammed with traffic during those hours, and even on the weekends. The expressway was the gateway from New Jersey into the outer boroughs of Brooklyn, Queens and suburban Long Island. Who would want to pass through Manhattan to get into these areas unless you were coming from Upper Jersey by the George Washington Bridge or from Connecticut or Upstate New York, in which case you'd be cutting through the Bronx? The South Shore of the Island, once quiet and peaceful, was rapidly becoming overdeveloped.

The Staten Island Mall, farm area at one time, had become a veritable landscape of shopping centers, condos and apartment complexes. The areas north of my neighborhood of Rosebank — Stapleton, St. George and Tompkinsville — had succumbed to urban blight. The Park Hill section of Clifton had become notorious for crime in the '80s and was derisively known by other Islanders as "Crack Hill." Other North Shore areas such as Mariner's Harbor, West Brighton and Stapleton had fallen to the crack epidemic that ran rampant through inner-city neighborhoods.

Residents in white Staten Island were wary of these areas. There were some who grew up in these aforementioned neighborhoods and viewed the changes firsthand when the population changed from white to black/Hispanic in the '60s and '70s. Or the majority of Staten Island residents were native Brooklynites who once lived in slum areas such as Brownsville/East New York and viewed the deterioration of these neighborhoods firsthand.

The neighborhood I lived in, Rosebank, was mostly Italian-American with a smattering of Irish-Americans. Rosebank had

an old world Italian flavor about it, especially off the streets of
Tompkins Avenue. Old women would sit out on the stoops, mon-
itoring the activities of the neighborhood, and the retired men
would sit outside the local delis, keeping up with all the gossip.

Locals were mostly suspicious of outsiders. Even as late as the
1980s, there was an unwritten code that if you were in a neighborhood other than your own, you'd best get the hell out of there.
Otherwise, you would risk catching a beating. That same code
held true for the black areas of Stapleton/Park Hill. If a white face
was walking along Vanderbilt Avenue, do not think for a moment
that no action would be taken. Residents of neighborhoods were
territorial, and if you didn't belong, you stayed in your own neighborhood. Howard Beach, the close-knit Italian-American community in Queens whose most famous resident was mob boss John
Gotti, certainly followed that code. I'm referring to that unfortunate incident where a gang of whites chased a group of young
black males out of the neighborhood with baseball bats, causing
them to flee across the Belt Parkway, where one of them was killed
by an oncoming car. That incident became etched throughout the
city and nation. Two years later, tensions were still raw between
the races.

I never cared for that "code." Why couldn't I walk where I
wanted to walk? Sometimes, exploring a different neighborhood
could be fascinating. There was always that imaginary border that
you didn't cross from Rosebank into Clifton on Tompkins Avenue,
which was the salt mine. It was also vice versa for Clifton residents,
unless you were shopping at the A&P. I would cross that border to
get to the Colonial Lanes Bowling Alley or to see Killian, but that
wasn't too deep into the Clifton area.

I was curious, but I wasn't brave enough to be a pioneer and
charter new frontiers into an unknown area. I liked having my
head attached to my body — and to think I almost had it detached.

It was truly a great day for me to be back among friends. Rob
was his usual, druggy, dopey self. Erika and I asked him about
Woodstock, but the fool couldn't remember who was on the bill
that day. "Jimi Hendrix played there? Oh, shit!"

"Rob, how much shit did you do that weekend?" Erika demanded to know. "What *do* you remember?"

"Mud, man, mud! That rain kept coming down."

"How did you survive three days in the mud?" she asked. "What the hell did you people do for food?"

"The Army copters. They flew in the food. That was far out." Amazingly, Rob could remember something about Woodstock other than mud and rain.

The irony of all this wasn't lost on me. "Holy cow, isn't it ironic that that the U.S. Army caters in food for the very same people protesting them and their actions in Vietnam?"

"Yeah, good one, Roddy," Erika agreed. "You hippies were so stoned, you didn't even think about food."

"Smart-ass kids," Rob snorted. "You think you know everything."

Shoes That Do Not Fit

Despite my happiness at being back at the record shop, I was still unsettled about traveling into Manhattan. I always had that feeling of being followed. Who would jump me this time? Was it paranoia brought on by the mugging? Perhaps, but what happened was all too real and quite hard to shake.

I decided, against my better judgment, to look for another job. My aunt was suggesting Starlite Home Center, so I decided to apply. Within a week's time, I was hired as a stock boy. The fact that I was hired rather quickly should have been an ominous sign. I needed a car in order to get there, so my aunt gladly lent me the use of her '86 Nissan Sentra. She worked during the day, so my job called for me to work on weekends and a few weeknights. My sprained wrist was healing up nicely, and it wouldn't hamper my abilities to perform the job. The duties required were stocking shelves, sweeping up the floor, cleaning out the toilets and helping customers with any heavy merchandise they wanted to load into their vehicles.

The tasks required weren't an issue; but a night manager named Humphrey, who seemed to delight in specializing as a prick, became my issue. It was because of him that my demise at the job happened in my second week.

My ouster from the job occurred on a Friday evening, when I was asked to stay late because there was a sick call. I agreed against my better judgment, and I paid heavily for it. I was abused heavily by "Hump-phrey," especially when it came to collecting shopping carts in that humongous parking lot, and that February evening was quite chilly, in the 20s.

"Hurry up, McPherson," Hump-phrey barked. "Get a move on! Let's go!" He was a young guy, only 10 years older than I, but very uptight and a ball breaker. Let's get this shit wrapped up outside already. You still have plenty of work to do. Chop chop! Let's go!"

I was really hurt by this prick's attitude, and it was then I started to sorely miss Rob, Erika and the record shop. Erika was really upset that I was leaving, but Rob, in a surprising moment of clarity, predicted I would be back. "Give him three weeks," he insisted.

"Oh, shouldn't we throw a party for him?" Erika pleaded.

"For what? He'll be back."

As I was pushing the carts to the front of the store, I saw Hump-phrey laughing at my misfortune while on a cigarette break. I was winded after having traversed the whole parking lot in gathering up shopping carts. With the lasting adrenaline I still had, I ran those carts to the front of the store as fast as I could, and Hump-phrey was in the line of fire. While barking orders at me, he was out on his cigarette break, and he had the nerve to ask me earlier in the day to take only a half-hour break. I'm glad I took a full hour, because if I hadn't, I would have had no energy to spare. He didn't seem to notice I was gone for the full hour, but I could give a rat's ass for his feelings; there was no consideration for mine. Even after that "break" episode and his abuse during the past two weeks, I wanted to like him, but his overbearing attitude made it impossible to tolerate him any longer.

How could I forget how the prick delighted in giving me orders during the day before he asked me to stay on, due to a sick call. "Okay, Roddy, what I need you to do is clean out the bathrooms. They are a pig sty. Then I need you to empty out all the garbage cans by the cash registers. Make sure the compactor is cleared of trash. Then I need you to run any stock to the shelves that need restocking."

A customer, a New York Jets jersey-wearing fan in his mid-30s, overheard this exchange and marveled at Hump-phrey's audacity. "Why don't you stick a pencil in his ear?" he told me. That comment had me in stitches.

I wasn't laughing while pushing the carts in the freezing cold, although my adrenaline and anger were keeping me warm. The bastard never knew he was going to be the target of my wagons. He just turned his head for a few seconds to flick his ashes from his cigarette, but that's all it took for flesh and metal to meet. Hump-phrey fell hard to the ground.

My victim lay on the ground all crumpled up, holding his groin area and in obvious pain. A few customers walking in and out of the store were horrified by this display of violence. I simply looked down at Hump-phrey, uttered the words "I quit" and walked off to my car.

Aunt Jane was displeased with me that night when I came home. "Have ye lost your mind? Couldn't ye have talked with him?"

"He was a sonuvabitch! You can't reason with him. I helped him out because the night person called in sick, and here I am, killing myself, and he's abusing me. I don't have to take that abuse. Haven't I been through enough?"

My voice was animated, and I was highly upset. I never really wanted to work in this job, and I had taken it only because it was closer to home. It was a shitty job compounded by a shitty boss with no compassion.

My aunt saw how upset I was, and she didn't argue with me any further. "It's all done now. What are ye going to do for a job?"

"The Country Club Diner at Clove Road is hiring busboys. I'll apply there."

My aunt nodded in approval. "At least ye still close to home."

That's all she seemed to care about, that I was closer to home. I really wanted to call Rob and tell him I was ready to come back to the Den. I really had no desire to work in a restaurant environment. But I knew my aunt wouldn't let up on me, so I went to apply for the job the next day.

The manager, a fat guy with a mustache and in his late 40s, looked me over. "Yes, we need a lot of help. Are you still in school?"

"Yeah."

"Are you able to work nights and weekends?"

"I can work to a certain time on weeknights, until 10 p.m. But Saturday nights are not a problem. I can work Sundays during the day."

"Great," the manager enthused. "Can you start tomorrow?"

The offer took me by surprise. I started on Monday night. I would be working Monday nights, Wednesday nights, Friday nights, Saturday nights and Sunday from late morning to late afternoon. I was told to wear black slacks and a white shirt; fortunately, I had both in my possession. Management gave me a cheesy red dinner jacket and a clip-on bow tie to complete the outfit. To say I disliked this particular job would be an understatement. I couldn't stand it! The managers were overbearing, particularly the fat mustachioed guy, Mario. The waitresses were mainly middle-aged grumpy women who were plainly miserable for whatever reason. And the customers? Once you put on that red jacket, it was an open invitation to be treated like shit. This was indentured servitude.

"Excuse me, I need more water." "Excuse me, I never got bread." "Where's my soup?" "I need a fork and knife. How can I eat this, with my hands?" "There's something floating in my glass!" "Kid, where's my waitress? I need the check; I've got to go!"

If it was a busy night, you couldn't move fast enough to clear the tables. I didn't experience the full craziness of this diner until Friday night. Holy Mother of God, the people kept streaming in. You had the dinner crowd after 5 p.m., which consisted of parents with their bratty kids climbing all over the tables. And while the kids were acting up, the idiotic parents were pleading with them: "Now Anthony, you must sit still." The kids are whining: "Wahhhhh, wahhhhhh!" And then you had the manager, exhorting me to clear the tables faster: "I have a party of six coming in. Let's go!"

It dawned on me that I was the only white guy performing this task of the lowly busboy. The others were Mexican. They were pleasant enough, but barely knew English. I'm sure their status in the country was illegal, but I marveled at their work ethic. This was the kind of work ethic America had back during the Depression era and World War II. They had no choice but to work their ass off since they wanted to be in this country, or if they were sending money back home. I had the work ethic, but I didn't have the high tolerance for abuse that the Mexicans did. They didn't have a choice; I did. Friday and Saturday nights were the huge dinner crowds followed by the 11 p.m. and after crowd, which consisted of people coming off from the movies or bar-hopping. It was another reason to resent this job. I was only a 17-year-old with no life except work, and I was really regretting leaving the record shop. I was working for a piddling $2 an hour. What a disgrace!

It all came to a head on Sunday morning when dealing with the brunch crowd. It was a bit ridiculous getting off at midnight and having to come back to work at 10 o'clock in the morning. Even my aunt thought this was over the top. But I went in later that morning, toughing it out.

The Sunday morning group was a rough crowd, even tougher than the recovering drunks of Friday and Saturday night. One old-timer was upset at me for not getting his coffee fast enough, and I wasn't even the waiter. "Can't you get any faster than that?"

"Yo!" a guidette called out. "We need some water here."

Where were the manners? Whatever happened to "please" and "thank you"?

A 40-ish guy caught my attention. "We need bread here. We've been waiting 10 minutes for it."

I went back into the kitchen, grabbed a pitcher of water and a loaf of bread. Enough was enough. The guy whining about the bread was the first one I approached. "Here's your goddamned bread!" I snarled as I tossed it hard at his chest.

"Hey!" exclaimed the startled man. "What the hell!"

And then I approached the guidette eating her brunch with her equally doofus boyfriend. I proceeded to spill the contents of the pitcher onto her head. She shrieked loudly at the coldness of the liquid, and I tossed the empty pitcher onto the table in front of her surprised boyfriend.

The buffoon was incensed. "Da fuck ya doin' man? You lookin' to get your ass kicked in?" He stood up waiting to pound my head.

"Why don't you shut the fuck up and sit down! Finish your fuckin' breakfast!" I brandished the empty water pitcher as a weapon. "Lay a hand on me and you are as good as dead!"

A giant hush fell over the Sunday brunch crowd. Those who were fighting hangovers from last night's/this morning's previous activities had to have been sobered up by now. I had become the main performer, center stage. The doltish boyfriend started to walk over to me, but Mario stepped in between us. "What the hell are you doing?" he demanded of me.

"I quit!" I yelled as I tossed the water pitcher to the floor. I then took off my red jacket and threw it down. For a grand finale, I shouted at the top of my lungs: "Fuck it!" and walked out of the diner.

"That kid is nuts," I heard the boyfriend exclaim.

Back at home, Aunt Jane, of course, was incredulous. "Two jobs in three weeks? I don't believe ye! I really don't believe ye! What has crawled into your noggin'? Did those muggers brain damage ye?"

"I'm going back to the record shop. I was happy there. If you don't like it, Aunt Jane, you can toss me out of the house. I really don't care."

"For crying out loud, just go back," she gave in. "Ye were happy there, but I don't understand the attraction with that bloody shop. Ach, ye skull is so thick. And this city isn't safe anymore. I hate ye traveling."

"I'll watch myself," I promised. "Do you think I want that to happen to me again?"

Teacher Troubles

During this time, my troubles with Mr. Crano intensified. It was clear I was no artist, and my inability to perform an exercise in class triggered an outburst from him that was over the top and out of line.

"You stupid moron, you stupid bastard! What in the hell is wrong with you? Are you missing brains? Why are you so goddamned stupid? All you have to do is follow the coordinates on the paper. A simpleton can follow this. You're worse than a simpleton. You're hopeless!"

It was more than I or any other reasonable person should have to tolerate. I leapt out of the chair and shouted out to him, "Go fuck yourself!" The class, like the diner patrons on the day I quit, all hushed. Crano's mouth dropped to the floor.

I grabbed my book bag and stormed out of the room. "Hey, get back here!" Crano shouted, but I sure as hell wasn't stopping. Why do people yell that out? Do they think that person is going to listen and stop?

I was going off to the guidance counselor's office to get a program change. You'd have to be a fool or a masochist, possibly both, to stay in that class.

On my way, who should appear but a security officer, a crusty old woman named Andrea.

"Why are you out of class?" she demanded. "Where's your program card?"

I have heard stories about this old roly-poly security guard and how she was always chasing down delinquent kids who were roaming the hallways or trying to cut out of school. I was in no mood for any more fascistic behavior. Hadn't I just left a classroom taught by a fascist?

Andrea was coming from my left side, and her orders for me fell on deaf ears. I simply wasn't stopping for her. She wouldn't have listened to my side of the story. Most adults listened to teenagers' stories with cynicism. But I knew myself; I had never cut a single class in my whole time at this institution. Would it matter with this fake policewoman?

My walking pace increased, which angered Andrea. "You son of a — get back here now!" Her footsteps quickened behind me.

I broke into a run and made a beeline for the nearest stairwell. Andrea was yelling into her walkie-talkie for help. The whole structure of Normand High School was akin to a prison, where students were kept inside until the release times of 2:30 to 3 o'clock. You weren't even allowed outside for lunch, whereas in grammar school you were at least allowed off the premises for lunch.

I slammed through the stairwell door as I raced up the stairs. The objective was to reach the guidance counselor's office, which was on the third floor. Unfortunately, I was in the South Wing and the guidance counselor's office was in the North Wing. There was a good chance I would get nabbed before I reached my destination.

In retrospect, it was rather stupid for me to run; I could have held my ground and explained to Andrea what had happened, but I wasn't in the mood to explain. I was embarrassed and hurt by that son of a bitch Hitler type masquerading as a teacher. Hitler was a failed commercial artist, and so was Crano. But Crano hadn't taken over any countries and demolished certain segments of their populations. He was just an abusive old man to his students.

I reached the third floor, and all was quiet in the South Wing until I exited out of there. Lo and behold, I came across another security guard walking toward me, a tall, thin woman in her late 40s.

I saw her and immediately made a beeline for the West Wing on my right side — not where I wanted to be, but I had no choice. I heard the security guard screaming at the top of her lungs imploring me to stop, and she was hauling ass. She was pretty quick for an older woman, but I was faster. My options were running low as I made my way toward another stairwell. I wound up on the second floor of the West Wing, and coming at me from my left was a younger security guard, a black woman in her late 20s who had the speed of a gazelle. I turned up the juice and headed back for the stairwell. The trouble was that this security guard was gaining ground fast, and I almost tripped as I turned around. I quickly righted myself and then skipped up the steps in order to increase my distance from my gazelle-like pursuer. Unfortunately, who should be headed straight on down the stairs but the tall, thin, 40-ish security guard. It looked as if I was caught for sure, but I managed to fake her out by ducking under her grasp. The gazelle running behind me was attempting to grab me as well, but she wound up crashing into her partner. Both fell on the steps. I crashed hard myself through those stairwell doors and hightailed it to the North Wing. And wouldn't you know that Andrea was lurking about.

"Fuck," I muttered to myself. The chase was still on, and these people were harder to shake off than leeches. At least they tried to do their job well.

"Stop, goddamnit, stop!," Andrea yelled, but those words were lost on me. I lost her and approached the guidance counselor's door. I tried it, and the damn thing was locked.

"Shit!" I cursed. This chase was all for naught, and now the old lady was catching up to me with a sudden burst of speed. My lungs were aching, so I started to run again on pure adrenaline. I rounded the corner, losing sight of Andrea, and ducked into a darkened classroom where a film was being shown. It was *One Flew Over the Cuckoo's Nest* with Jack Nicholson. All eyes were riveted on the screen, and no one noticed when I plopped my rear end down in an empty seat. I put my head down on the desk and watched Randall P. McMurphy and his fellow psych ward inmates agitate Nurse Ratched as they pretended to watch a baseball game on a blank TV screen and have a great time. I also heard Andrea's walkie-talkie crackle with static as she was trying in vain to find me.

I stayed and watched the film until the dismissal bell sounded. As the students filed out of the room, I did my best to merge in with them. Before I could file out, I heard a familiar voice.

"Roddy?"

It was unmistakable. I whirled around, and the voice belonged to my favorite teacher, Brenda Moriarty.

"Oh, hi," I said nervously. "Great movie or what? I'll see you next class."

"No, no, not so fast, young man. I want to talk to you."

I stopped for her. She had caught me, and I was involving her in this mess, too.

"What's going on with you?" Brenda persisted.

"I'm watching a movie, that's all."

"What class are you supposed to be in?"

"Art."

"And why weren't you there?"

"Because Mr. Crano and I don't get along. He hates me. I screwed up an assignment, and he started lacing into me. He called me a stupid bastard and said that I was hopeless. So I walked out of there."

Brenda's eyes widened. "Oh, my God, Roddy. Are you serious?"

"Yeah." I was doing my best not to cry, but because someone was asking me this and I was really hurt by Crano's verbal abuse, a tear came to my eye.

"That's terrible," Brenda said, stating the obvious. "Did you try going to your guidance counselor?"

"I did, but the security guards were chasing me all over the building. I wound up in here to hide out."

Brenda was perplexed. "Why were the security guards chasing after you? Didn't you try to explain to them what was happening?"

"No, the guards wouldn't care."

Brenda shook her head and laughed in an "I don't believe it" kind of fashion. "You could have at least tried. I'm sure they would have understood. But your running away like that makes you look guilty as if you were cutting class. You really need to talk to your guidance counselor tomorrow."

"I want to."

Just then, the security guards burst into the room. "There he is," Andrea pointed out. "We have been looking all over for him. Come, young man, you're going to the dean's office!"

"Ladies, I know the whole story," Brenda explained. "He wasn't cutting class; he's having problems with his last period teacher. The teacher was verbally abusive to him, and he stormed out."

"Well, why couldn't he tell us that?" Andrea wondered.

"He doesn't trust adults too well. Would you when a teacher calls you a stupid bastard?" Brenda asked rhetorically.

The black security guard, younger and less cynical than Andrea, mouthed "Damn, is that true?"

I nodded, but as much as I appreciated Brenda sticking up for me, it was embarrassing to have this dirty linen aired out for public consumption, which was part of the reason why I didn't tell them.

"He was ashamed, and can you blame him for not wanting to tell you? But you are sorry for running them ragged like that, aren't you, Roddy?"

"Yeah."

Even Andrea lightened up. "Next time, please tell us. Don't run away like that. You almost gave me a heart attack."

The black security guard, whose nameplate read "Connie," wished me luck. Then she added, "You should try out for the track team." They left the room kids started to file in for the next class.

Brenda breathed a sigh of relief. "You are so lucky, Roddy. Please go to the guidance counselor's office tomorrow."

"I will," I said with a nod, "and can I ask you a favor?"

"What is it?"

"Can you take me in your film and literature class?"

I did visit the guidance counselor's office the following day during my lunch period. Mr. Scolari was a youthful, pleasant-faced preppie guy. He agreed that a change should be made. I lobbied for Brenda's film and literature class, but I had already taken that course in sophomore year under another teacher, so that was out. The only other class that was open was typing. It didn't seem such a bad choice. I fancied myself somewhat of a writer. And typing would obviously be beneficial. That change became effective immediately that day, so I didn't have to look at that bastard Crano's puss anymore.

The typing teacher, Mrs. Welsh, a lady closing in on her 60s, was not too thrilled about receiving another student in her class.

"Tsk, tsk, I don't know why they do this to me. You're a few weeks behind already, so you have to catch up."

"That's not a problem," I said to her in earnest. "I want to learn." For the most part, the students spent most of the class time practicing typing. Mrs. Welsh had two rules for the class: never look at the keyboard while typing and never chew gum. I could understand the rule about chewing gum. You may get some slob who spits it out accidentally into the typewriter and then that machine is ruined.

The no-looking-at-the-keyboard rule, however, I violated. On my second day in that class, Mrs. Welsh came around with her black book and red pen making notes about anyone violating her rules.

"Coletti," she barked at a female student. "Spit that gum out! You know the rules already. Why are some people so bubble-headed?"

"McPherson, stop looking at the keyboard. I told you yesterday we don't do that here."

"Yes, ma'am," I answered.

I exchanged one hard ass for another, but at least she wasn't insulting like Crano, except if you were chewing gum, which you really couldn't blame her for getting upset about.

The Holdup

I couldn't believe the drama I was experiencing in my senior year. It was as if I was trying to make up for three years of boredom, with the exception of my Uncle Harry passing away the previous spring.

But other than that, I led a rather boring life. It was a rather beautiful March Sunday, with a 60-degree temperature, and I had decided to take a walk down Bay Street through the Stapleton section. Bay Street was going through a renaissance during the late '80s with the addition of a new naval homeport. It was supposed to drum up business for the area, which had fallen on hard times back in the '70s; and it looked like with the addition of McDonald's and a few new clubs that it was starting to come back. I stopped inside a bodega to get a soda, and there were a few other patrons inside: a middle-aged Hispanic man, a younger Hispanic woman in her 20s and a black male about my age. As I was ready to go on line to pay for my Mountain Dew, two men with stocking caps over their heads and carrying shotguns burst into the place.

"All right, this is a stickup!" announced one of the gunmen. "Let's see the money, now!"

"Everyone on the floor except for you, pops," a gunman barked at the owner behind the counter, an elderly, heavyset Hispanic man.

All of us patrons emptied our pockets and got on the floor as quickly as we could.

"Oh my God, oh my God. We're going to die. *Dios mio!*" moaned the Hispanic woman.

"Shut up, bitch!" the other gunman yelled. "You're gonna get a bullet up your ass if you keep crying."

"Come on, pops," the first gunman yelled at the bodega owner, who stood frozen at the counter. "The money, now!"

I stared at the floor. Could this really be happening? We always read about and watch heists on the news. You also see re-creations of heists in TV dramas and movies. It is scary only when you are involved yourself. The guns are real, the voices are loud, the people around you are helpless and panicking. I just wanted this to be over. They could have my driver's license and my measly 20 dollars in the wallet.

I made the mistake of trying to catch a glance at the action. The second gunman was not happy about my curiosity. He slammed the butt of his rifle above my left eye. I saw stars, and a throbbing pain intensified. "Keep your head to the floor, mother fucker, or I'll blow it off," he roared.

The Hispanic woman was sobbing hysterically and praying in Spanish.

"Bitch, you're gonna get the same thing he got if you don't shut your ass up."

The first gunman was getting impatient with his partner. "Yo, can that shit. Just collect the money, and let's get the fuck out of here."

A deafening explosion followed. All of us looked up. You couldn't help yourself; the noise was so startling. The owner of the bodega had whipped out a pistol from under the counter and had shot the first gunman in the head. The gunman's body went sprawling into a display of Drake's cakes. The second gunman wasted no time in springing into action, and he shot the owner square in the chest. Blood literally exploded out of the man. The Hispanic woman was shrieking uncontrollably while the rest of us prayed that we wouldn't be next on the shooter's list. But as luck would have it, New York's Finest showed up in front of the store. I guess they were about to buy lunch at this very same place when the gunshots rang out. The two officers came blazing in with their .38s and shot the remaining gunman dead. He crashed back onto the floor, missing me by just inches.

"*Dios mio!*" shrieked the Hispanic woman.

I was shaking like a leaf. Those past five minutes had to be the most intense and scariest I had ever been through in my life. The cops saw I had been injured and had put in a request for a "bus." Blood was streaming into my eye, trickling from the gash above my eyebrow, which needed a few stitches. The ambulance came, and I visited the hospital for the second time in a month.

The wait at Bayley Seton Hospital was endless. I managed to get a cubicle while many patients sat in the waiting room, sick from flu. My aunt was called, and she was relieved as well as distressed. Relieved for me, because I was still alive. Distressed, no doubt, by seeing me injured again. She was crying and hugging me frantically.

"This Island is getting worse and worse. None of us are safe anymore."

That statement echoed the statement uttered by my mom in our Bronx apartment 11 years earlier, when we saw a battered Mrs. Finnigan being carried out on a stretcher.

"It's getting worse and worse," Aunt Jane muttered. "Why the hell were ye walking down there in Stapleton?" she demanded to know. "What's wrong with the candy stores in Rosebank? Ye have to go to Stapleton to buy a soft drink?" She's saying all of this as the doctor is tugging on the stitches above my eyebrow. That was painful, and the doctor's tugging along with my aunt's incessant nagging was driving me to distraction.

"Jesus, Aunt Jane, Stop! Please! The last thing I need is a lecture. What's done is done!"

I went home that afternoon, and I barely remember studying. The events at the bodega were prominent in my mind. And when I went to sleep that night, I had horrible nightmares of those gunmen, their stocking heads and their rifles. I saw these stocking-headed figures when I went to the bathroom in the middle of the night, just hovering over my bed and standing in the hallway leading off to the bathroom. They seemed so lifelike until I walked through them, and then I realized they were apparitions. They vanished when I turned on the bathroom lights. But as soon as I was finished in the bathroom, I turned off the lights and the figures reappeared. When I returned to my bedroom, I crawled back into bed with the nightlight on. It seemed rather inane to do that at my age, but that was the only way I could make the nightmares stop.

I was the talk of the school the following day. The stitches definitely got people's attention. The previous day's action had made the Sunday evening news, and it was a major story in the NYC newspapers. It was the top headline in the local newspaper, the *Staten Island Advance*. Students and teachers couldn't get enough of asking me about the robbery.

"Were you scared?" "Does the cut above your eye hurt?" That second question bordered on stupidity. You try getting slammed in the head by a rifle butt! I felt my brain shake a bit, and I was surprised I had all my marbles. I was also told by my doctor that I would have a permanent scar as a result. The one fact I could take solace in was that those two dregs were dead.

John Corsi marveled at my bad luck. "Are you a magnet for these scumbags? You've had your ass kicked a lot in school; now you're getting your ass kicked in the outside world."

"It's that 25 percent Irish luck," I quipped. "It follows me around."

Brenda asked me about my welfare almost every day. She had become a friend, but unlike other teachers, she would speak to me in private and not exclaim, "What happened to you?" like they all would in front of a bunch of gaping and gawking students.

"I was involved in a robbery a few years ago back at a Citibank in Brooklyn. I wasn't injured, but I was scared to death. You must have been terrified," she commented.

"I was, and I'm still terrified. I had nightmares last night."

"That's understandable," Brenda said, nodding. "So did I. If they don't go away, you should see a psychiatrist. I was able to shake it off a few days later, but some people never do."

It was ironic that week that Brenda happened to give us an assignment asking us students about the scariest experience we ever had. This was a tossup for me between the mugging and the bodega robbery. Even though I was injured a bit more severely in the mugging experience, it happened so fast, I never knew what hit me. With this bodega holdup, I was fully aware of what was going on with all that screaming and shooting. I'll never forget the deafening noise of those gun blasts. Not to mention the blood. The blood dripping down from my forehead, the blood on the walls, the blood on the floor, and the dead bodies of the bodega owner and the two gunmen. The noise level of guns is truly loud. Television does not do justice to the sound of guns.

After the assignment was read, Brenda exclaimed, "Oh, my God, that is so terrible!" And the rest of the class shook their heads in dismay.

Brenda apologized to me after the class for making me live through "it" again.

"I wanted to talk about it," I said. "It helped."

"I'm glad, but if you are ever uncomfortable with an assignment, just tell me."

It was nice having a teacher ask about my well being, rather than harassing me about a botched assignment or why I flubbed a math problem. Here was a teacher I totally trusted and felt at ease with. Why couldn't they all be like her?

Foiling a Robbery

The luck of the Irish in attracting dregs was still following me about the next weekend at the record shop. Rob had to run some errands while Erika and I held down the fort. I was in the midst of recounting the gory details to Erika when the phone rang, and I had to hold off on the conversation to take the call. A customer had called to see if we had a particular album in stock, and I had to get the backorder in the storeroom to see if we had that. While I was checking for the backorder list, I heard a loud male voice shout out, "All right, bitch, the money out of the drawer, now!" I sneaked a peek from the back room, and there was an unkempt, unshaven man in front of the counter, with a wild-eyed look and a gun dangling in front of an ashen-faced Erika.

"C'mon bitch, hurry up!" The wild-eyed man's shouts were becoming more frantic.

What I did next was either the bravest or the most foolish stunt I had ever committed. I crawled low along the record racks clutching the Louisville Slugger baseball bat that Rob kept on the premises for protection. When I was able to get close to the gunman, I took the bat and made the biggest swing I had ever made. I had never swung so hard in little league. My batting ability was as impressive as Ma Kettle shooing away the goats. The bat connected with the man's head, and the force of the blow knocked him to the ground. I followed up by jabbing him in the stomach and grabbed his pistol, which he had lost his grip on when I dealt him the first blow. I held the gun over him and yelled for Erika to call the cops. She did, and I stayed in that position above the man for 10 minutes. When it looked like he wasn't going to be reviving so fast, I put the gun on the counter and just stood over him with the bat.

The cops arrived with an ambulance in tow, and they took the robber to a hospital. The store was shut down for an hour while the cops took statements from me and Erika. Rob, "Johnny Come

Lately," walked into the midst of this and demanded to what was going on.

I was pissed off with him, because I knew exactly what errands he was running. He was out there scoring weed at Washington Square Park. But then again, how could a stoner like Rob protect us?

After the cops left, I laced into Rob for being so selfish. Erika and I were risking our lives for his business and he was out there scoring weed.

"Dude, you need to mellow out, man. You should try some of this." He held up one of the joints.

I shook my head in disgust. "I told you I don't touch that shit, Rob. Don't you fuckin' hear?"

"Easy, man, easy," Rob cautioned. "It's your loss. Erika, would you like to come into the back room?"

Poor Erika was still shaking. "Oh my God, I saw the bullets in the gun. They were there. Roddy was so brave to do what he did. He's a hero, Rob."

"Kid, I didn't think you had it in you," Rob commented. "You always seemed timid."

"Maybe the last few months changed me Rob," I said wearily.

Erika and Rob went off to the back room. After a couple of minutes, I went back there to head off to the restroom. Both were sitting there mellowing out on dime joints.

"Hey, Roddy, you sure you don't want to try?" Rob persisted.

I just shook my head at the toking duo. "I have to go to the bathroom."

After a minute, I came out. They were in bliss land. "Roddy, c'mon, try it," Rob exhorted.

Against my better judgment, I decided to take a toke.

"Inhale it man," Rob instructed. "You get the full effects that way."

There were no full effects from what I could tell. I passed the joint back to Rob.

"Somebody's got to mind the store. You two forgot about that, didn't you?"

"That's why you're here," Rob retorted.

"Asshole," I muttered as I walked back to the front.

My way of relaxing was putting on Yes's *Tales of Topographic Oceans*. It was atmospheric music. Rob and Erika had their medicine; ambient music by Brian Eno was mine. Erika and Rob came out of the back room, and both expressed their comments regarding the music.

"Good shit to listen to," Rob enthused. "Mellow out."

"What is this hippie music shit, Roddy?" Erika demanded. "Your tastes are so weird. Soundtracks, '70s funk, progressive rock. I don't get you. What the hell happened to U2?"

Erika was referring to my favorite band, U2, although I was fast losing interest in them. I had become a fan of U2 with the release of their *War* album five years prior. It was raw, aggressive, intense with some moments of beauty, such as the hymn-like last track, "40." Otherwise, you couldn't best U2 for their aggressiveness on such tracks as "Sunday Bloody Sunday," "New Year's Day," "Two Hearts Beat as One" and "Pride." With the release of *The Joshua Tree* in '87, U2 became the biggest band in the world. And Bono, the lead singer, was all over the press, expounding upon his beliefs.

He's well meaning, but the preachiness went over the top. Now everyone, even the nerds and jocks in school, were liking them. They didn't feel so special to me anymore, and I felt they were no longer my band.

Erika was totally into punk, so her tastes were different from mine, save for U2. This was the one band that we could agree on, although she claimed they had sold out with *Joshua Tree*. I didn't agree, although that post-punk aggressiveness that endeared me to them was gone. I didn't have much use for modern rock music, or much rock music at all. Other than U2, I did enjoy the sounds of The Beatles, Yes, Floyd and Genesis, but that was rock and roll of the past, not very current. Metal and punk, which were Killian's and Erika's favorite genres, respectively, smacked of redundancy. You heard one song of the genre, you heard them all. At least the progressive rock genre, as long-winded as some of the songs are, smacked of intelligence. But I wasn't so out of touch with the '80s music scene. I still listened to Top 40 radio; my current faves, U2; and you would find a decent song now and again. I would watch MTV occasionally. That's how I kept up with modern music.

Yes, it was true my musical tastes were not in keeping with the 1980s train of thought. However, I wasn't in a mood for musical critique. "It's better than that speed freak shit you listen to," I shot back at Erika. "Haven't you had enough fuckin' excitement for one day?"

After those 80 minutes of tranquility passed, a news reporter from the *New York Post* came into the shop. He was youthful looking, in his early 20s. The man reminded me of Jimmy Olson, the photographer from the *Superman* movies.

"Excuse me, but where can I meet a Roddy McPherson?"

"Right here," I answered.

"Oh, this is great," the reporter enthused. "Is it true you helped foil a robbery? That is incredibly great news. I heard about this on the police radio. New Yorkers are starved for good news in this city. Would you mind sitting down for an interview?"

I was reluctant. "No, I can't help you out." I didn't feel like making a spectacle out of myself, but Rob and Erika were badgering me.

"Do it," Rob encouraged. "It would be great publicity for the store."

"You're a hero, buddy!" Erika exclaimed.

I did the interview for 20 minutes. The reporter asked me questions about how I had stopped the wild-eyed man: Was I scared? Did I ever think for one moment that I could have been killed? These thoughts had never occurred to me. All I saw was that my friend Erika was in danger, and something snapped inside of me. I was tired of having maggots such as these freaks prey on me and others. I took a big risk in subduing that robber, because he could have spotted me first and shot me before I could crack his head with the bat. In retrospect, that was foolhardy, but all of us at one time or another have taken risks that have defied good sense and logic.

Would I have done things differently in retrospect? No, I would have done it again, because there comes a time where you get sick of being preyed upon. I was thoroughly sick of being a victim, and I hadn't liked seeing Erika victimized.

After the interview, the reporter assured me I would be in tomorrow's paper.

"You're a celebrity, now," Erika crowed.

A celebrity. This was a new thing for me, and it would be a strange sensation as this week merged into next week. The first strange experience of this celebrity status was that Erika was asking me about my plans for the evening.

"I'm meeting with a friend," I answered. It was Brian Killian. I was looking forward to seeing him since his life had been so busy with school, the band and his girlfriend, Tabitha. I wondered why Erika was asking me about my "plans." We were always courteous and polite to each other in the store, but we never associated together outside the shop. We had nothing in common other than working at the store.

Erika was a lead singer in a punk band called Catharsis, which was playing at a club on the Lower East Side called The Bowery Ballroom at 10 p.m.

"I know you're not into punk, Roddy, but you should really check out my band. Bring your friend along."

"Can I take a rain check on that, Erika?" I just wasn't in the mood to have my head slammed with noise, although it would have been intriguing to see Erika in action.

Erika wasn't offended. "Okay, suit yourself. But you could have a real great time tonight." Then she called out to Rob: "Are you going to come tonight?"

Rob chuckled. "No way, young lady! So I can see you sick punk kids vomit on each other? If you've seen it once, you've seen it all."

"Kiss my ass," was Erika's retort.

After Erika left, Rob took me aside. "That chick really likes you now. She wants you to come to her gig. She really digs you."

"Rob, shut up!"

"I'm serious, man. She likes you now. Between you and me, Erika was talking about you. She found you quite cute, but you were too quiet and uptight for her liking."

"Really?" That was surprising and nice to know. But I couldn't bring myself to believe it.

My perception of myself at that time was so shitty, I couldn't believe any girl could find me cute.

"Rob, I like Erika, but she and I are so different."

"Your loss, man. Your loss."

I left the shop to meet up with Killian in Chinatown, and to our later regret, we chose to eat at some dive basement restaurant. Usually in our conversations, I was the listener and Killian was the talker, since his life was far more interesting than mine. Talk would usually be about his band, his job or his girlfriend. But I held court that night with my experience earlier in the day.

"You actually did that!" Killian was amazed. "That takes balls. Holy shit! I can't wait to read about this!"

I was patting myself on the back, really feeling good about myself when I saw something brown scurry in a darkened corner of the restaurant. It was putting me off my beef lo mein and distracting me from my boasting.

"Oh, man, there's a roach," I moaned in disgust.

Killian was thrown off by my sudden diversion in conversation. "What? Stop joking, man."

"Asshole, it's in the corner, crawling around."

Killian craned his neck around to see the little bugger in the corner, and he winced at the sight. "Oh, fuck," the metal head moaned. "I think I'm going to be sick. And you had to show me that shit?"

We beat a hasty retreat out of that restaurant and walked through the streets of Chinatown, figuring out our next game plan for the evening. I suggested Erika's band, but Killian wanted no part of it.

"I've had enough of lousy bands. Our singer sucks, and our drummer blows." Killian was clearly amused with himself, and he started chuckling. "That's a great name for that team: Suck and Blow."

While I'm no musician, I often told Killian my opinion of the aforementioned duo. I just merely shrugged my shoulders this time.

"I have to get out of this band, Roddy. It's killing me. My ears are hurting."

I was perplexed. "Something wrong with your hearing?"

"Yeah, it's those blasts of horrible drumming from Dave. Why can't he be quiet like the audiences out there?"

"Why do you waste your time if you hate it so much?" I asked. "Leave."

"We're very popular on the Island. We have a gig lined up at one of the clubs on Bay Street in a couple of weeks, and better yet, we'll be playing at a punk fest at CBGB's next month."

"Well, it can't be all that bad."

"You're gonna come see us, right?" Killian asked hopefully.

"Of course," I answered. "What else would I be doing?" To tell you the truth, I had no desire to see his band so soon, and while he and the bass guitarist were good players, Killian wasn't lying about the singer and drummer. But what excuse did I have not to see his band?

"Let's catch a movie," Killian suggested.

We traveled up to the East Village area, where we saw *Die Hard* with Bruce Willis.

Neither of us was a big Bruce Willis fan, but he made a really credible action hero. Alan Rickman was a fantastic villain. The special effects and stunts were amazing. It was one of the better action movies I had ever seen.

"Yippie ki-yay," uttered Killian as we walked out of the theater. He was mimicking protaganist John McClane's signature expression throughout the movie. "Yippie ki-yay," I muttered back. But as impressive as the movie was, it couldn't compete with the real live action I had seen earlier. Close but no cigar.

Hero

I told my Aunt Jane about the events the next morning. But even before I could do so, she let me know that she wasn't happy with me wandering in after midnight without a phone call.

"How do I know if yer not lying dead someplace," she lectured. "We've been through this already. I know yer head is thick, but let some sense wander through for once. Call if ye going to be out late!"

I apologized, and then I recounted the prior day's events. She was startled to hear of this, and even more startled to learn I was heroic but also stupid.

"My God, what in the hell is wrong with ye? Ye must have a death wish. What goes on with yer mind? Have those muggings and robberies damaged yer noggin? Ye don't take on a drug addict with a gun. Ye must not want to live. God in heaven, if yer mother didn't die back then, ye would have been the death of her now. For the love of God, stop being so stupid and give up the money! That roach-infested rat hole isn't worth yer life."

I understood where Aunt Jane was coming from. It was foolish to do that I had done, but the only person who got hurt, and deservedly so, was the wild-eyed gunman. I told Aunt Jane about the events because she was sure to read about them in the Sunday *Daily News*, which we subscribed to.

The *Staten Island Advance* sent a reporter over named Maureen Steinhagen, a really pleasant lady in her late 20s who really relaxed me for the interview. She was pretty, which also didn't hurt. She asked me if I was ever frightened for my life when I was trying to disarm the criminal.

"Yeah, but I've been victim of violent crime already. These creeps are killing us, literally."

Ms. Steinhagen asked me about other matters, such as school and what my plans were after high school.

"I really don't know yet," I answered, and I didn't. But in order to placate her and my aunt, I said, "College, but I'm not sure which field I want to take up."

"Do you consider yourself a hero?" Ms. Steinhagen asked.

"I'm no one special," I said. "I never was."

Ms. Steinhagen disagreed. She shook her head and smiled. "Your story is special, Roddy. Not many people could have been as brave as you were. You are special."

"Don't let it get to your noggin," my aunt's quick reply came. Good old Aunt Jane, always ready to keep me grounded and humble.

That was not the end of it. More news trucks came down our block. WNEW, WCBS, WABC, WNBC, WINS, WPIX. All local New York stations. I was a hero, like it or not. Aunt Jane was definitely not liking this media circus, but she had to live with it.

They all came to the front door with their flashing bulbs, cameras and microphones. I was asked the same questions as Ms. Steinhagen's, but these were more forceful and came at me in rapid fire. An impromptu press conference was held at my front door with my ever vigilant aunt watching from behind.

After a few questions, I broke it off. "I really need to study," I announced, shutting the door behind me.

My aunt sighed a breath of relief. "Good move, son." She hugged me and added, "I am proud of ye, Roddy, and I only scold so much because I love ye. Please don't do that again. You're young and need to live yer life. Your mother and father never got that chance."

The following Monday of school was full of praises for me.

"Hey, nice going!"

"God, that was so brave!"

"That wasn't you, was it?"

"This is not a joke, right?"

"That was really cool what you did. I could never do that."

It was rather nice to hear all of those comments, and I didn't realize that many people knew who I was. I thought my low, rather quiet profile kept me off the map, but I guess I was wrong.

The boys at the lunch table, Aquino, Castigelli and McMahon, couldn't stop talking about the incident. "Weren't you shitting bricks?" they asked.

John Corsi marveled at me. "Are you making up for all those years of not fighting back? But you're also crazy. You could have been shot!"

Now Corsi definitely could fight. He was shorter than me, but he could use his fists well. A lot of people underestimated him, but I've seen him take on bigger opponents and pulverize the shit out of them. There was one kid who was antagonizing him last year, and Corsi just reared back after taking all he could take and bloodied the kid's face. That was impressive. And he was the voice of sanity in this case. "Why the hell are you messing with a drug addict?"

Girls who had never given me the time of day went up and said, "Hi, I read about what you did. That is so amazing, so brave." I was uncomfortable with that and I had no experience with girls, except for the ones who genuinely liked me such as Louise Meyers, even during my days when I was a punching bag.

"Roddy, that is so brave, but you took some chance. I would hate to see anything happen to you. You're really a sweet guy," she stated.

All my teachers commented on my actions as brave and "incredible." One was guarded, and that was my favorite, Brenda Moriarty. She addressed me after class as she always did: "You are one crazy kid. Congratulations, young man, but please do not do that again. Your life is not worth getting risked over a record store."

I was touched by Brenda's sentiment, because I knew she was genuine.

"Roddy, I'm quite happy for you. You deserve this attention, because it takes a special person to do what you did, but you could have gotten yourself hurt or killed. Your life matters too."

I had operated under the attitude that I never counted for much, so who would care if I was gone?

"Well, your aunt would," Brenda pointed out. "Other family members would. Your friends at the record shop would be affected. And so would I. You're a good person."

I didn't know what to say. I was floored, and Brenda's comments were the best compliments I had received, other than Aunt Jane's.

St. Patrick's Day

I'm mostly Scottish, with 25 percent Irish blood. My ancestors were descendants from the Northern Highlands in Scotland. But the 25 percent Irish blood was enough for me to claim that I am Irish, not to mention the freckles on my cheeks, along with the slight auburn head of hair. I felt this was justification for me to take St. Patrick's Day as a personal day for myself and experience the parade.

I've always seen bits and pieces of it on TV, but TV never does it justice. This was an opportunity to take a mental health day, and with all that had gone on for me during that time, I felt I deserved it.

Even though spring was around the corner, and it had warmed up close to the 70-degree range just a few days earlier, the mercury suddenly dipped back toward the 40s for today. I was dressed in my leather bomber jacket with an Irish sweater underneath and a wool shirt underneath that one, yet I was still cold.

The wind chill felt as if it was in the 30s. I left home without a hat and soon regretted it, for even though my ears were covered by my hair, they were ringing with the cold. Fortunately, one of the many stands selling Irish souvenirs was hawking those Kelly berets, and I soon purchased one. Looking over everyone else's shoulders was no easy feat since there were already crowds of people decked out in green clothing, green plastic shamrocks, tricolor armbands or those cheesy "Kiss Me, I'm Irish" buttons. I was one of them with that button myself.

What were the odds that a tall, lanky lady with reddish hair covered by a green beret, blue eyes and smile sparking would come up next to me. All those characteristics were unmistakable.

"Well, it looks as if I'm not the only one who decided to cut class," the attractive woman joked.

"Ahh, shit," I groaned. "I'm busted."

"Don't sweat it, sweetie," Brenda Moriarty laughed. "Your secret is safe with me. Do you think I want anyone finding out I'm here too?"

I breathed a sigh of relief.

"Sometimes you need a mental health day. This is an annual ritual for me. I'm sure you never abuse cutting school. Is this the first time you've cut class other than being sick?"

I was blown away by her perceptiveness. "Yeah, how did you know that?

Brenda smiled. "My first St. Patrick's Day parade in Manhattan wasn't until I was about your age, maybe a little younger. I was always fascinated by what I saw on TV, but I never got a chance to see it in person." There was a slight pause and Brenda caught my button. "Oh, I don't mind if I do." She planted a kiss on my cheek.

"I never knew you were Irish, Roddy. I thought you were Scottish with a name like Roddy McPherson."

"There's about 25 percent Irish in me on my Mom's side," I said.

"That's good enough for me," Brenda said with a wink. "I told you already that I'm half-Scottish."

We viewed the pageantry for a couple of hours with the high school marching bands, the politicos and the many civil service workers of cops and firemen walking up Fifth Avenue, basking in the cheers of the crowd. Brenda was a hearty supporter, whooping it up with loud cheers; but her biggest cheers were reserved for her firefighter brother, who happened to work for Rescue 5 on Staten Island.

"Hey, there's my brother, Roddy. Hey, Jimmy! Over here!"

A tall, pleasant-looking guy broke out of marching ranks and ran over to Brenda. They embraced.

"Hiya, Sis, try to stay warm. It's freakin' cold out here!"

"Jimmy, you nut, why did you stop marching? Get back out there!" Brenda laughed.

"Okay, Sis, remember where we'll meet. See ya!"

We watched the tall figure go back to marching with his squad. People around us were laughing, because it was comic relief from the solemn, serious side of the parade. Here a firefighter broke ranks just to hug his sister.

The cold winds were still biting, despite the sun, and even Brenda had her limits after two hours.

"Let's get something to eat," she suggested.

We managed to get to an Irish pub a couple of blocks away called the Lucky Shamrock. The place was crowded, but we managed to get a table right away. Brenda treated me to lunch and wouldn't take no for an answer.

"Doesn't it feel good to get away for a day?" Brenda smiled brightly at me.

"I needed a mental health day," I explained. "I'm tired of teachers abusing me, and I'm tired of being asked about my injuries and this newspaper stuff. These people don't respect me. I'm talking about the kids in school. Now, all of a sudden, I'm worth something?"

"High school is fickle, Roddy. Someday you'll make friendships that are lasting and rewarding."

Even at 1 in the afternoon, the Lucky Shamrock was raucous. Men were downing pints of Guinness like big, behemoth cars of the '70s were guzzling gasoline. And most patrons were singing the song "Danny Boy" at the top of their lungs.

"Oh my God, I hate this song, and I'm part Irish too," Brenda moaned.

"What music do you like?" I asked.

"I'm into mostly '70s rock and roll. There are some bands I like today. U2 are pretty good. The Bangles are a good group. What about you?"

"I'd rather not say. You'd probably laugh."

"Wait a minute, you are not getting off that easy. I told you my tastes. You could at least tell me yours."

"Well, I like the Beatles, McCartney, the progressive stuff like Genesis, ELP, Yes. But I'm not into punk so much."

"You're looking at a huge Beatles fan. Particularly Paul McCartney. I saw Wings back in '76. That was a concert highlight for me."

I was floored. "You saw McCartney live? This is way too cool!"

"That was a great concert, a once-in-a-lifetime experience. You were talking about punk and how you are not into it? I just love all of that punk stuff," Brenda enthused. "I was a huge punk fan in my late teens. I guess it was my own rebellion. I had the purple dyed hair, the vampire makeup. It was so unique and different, although my mom was confused by it all. The Buzzcocks, the Sex Pistols, the Clash, Siouxsie and the Banshees. Siouxsie had really great style! And the music wasn't really polished, but that's the charm of it. But I did like those progressive bands too. Genesis is my favorite. I caught *The Lamb lies Down on Broadway* tour, which was Peter Gabriel's last one before Phil Collins took over for *A Trick of the Tail*. Now, that album I love. One of my top 10 albums. And the tour was excellent too!"

"Did you see any other bands?" I asked.

"There are so many to name. Regarding the bands you like, I saw Yes on their *Going for the One* tour. That was a good show, and it was with a revolving stage. I even saw Emerson, Lake and Palmer at Madison Square Garden with an orchestra. They were really good. That was the night of the famous '77 blackout, when there was a lot of looting. But, fortunately, I was in the one of the safest places. Getting home was so chaotic. Lots of people were out there in the streets. It was one huge party, but my mom was worried to death about me."

"I saw ELP with Cozy Powell two years ago at the Meadowlands," I enthused. "That was a great concert."

"So did I! What a small world. We were both in the same place. That was a great concert. Greg Lake is a really good singer. His voice is so commanding. That concert was a pick-me-up. I was going through the aftermath of a divorce, so that night was a lone bright spot for me during a terrible time."

I was taking it all in. Not only was my teacher a heavy advocate of creative writing, but she was a music lover too.

"Watch this," Brenda announced. She took a napkin and her own pen and drew a perfect replica of the Yes band's Roger Dean logo.

"Here, it's all yours."

I was really impressed. "Thank you. This is really special."

"My pleasure."

"Did you know that I work at a record shop?" I asked.

"I do. I was reading about that in one of the articles detailing your heroics. That is so cool. I have to make a trip one day to check it out, but life gets very busy at times."

After lunch, I decided to split. Brenda was going to meet up with her brother and hang out in the city. I hadn't told Aunt Jane that I was going to the St. Paddy's parade, and I doubt she would be happy with me if she found out. I wanted to get home before she did, which would be by 5 o'clock. I didn't really want to go home, though, and I wish I could have held onto that day. It was the best one I had in a long time.

A Good Deed Goes Punished

There was a girl in my creative writing class, Tammy Brascia, who sat one seat ahead of me. She was a 5-foot-5 cutie with brown curly hair, a cherubic face and doe-like brown eyes. Her personality seemed to be sweet and easygoing. And she always complimented me on my writing, especially how I was describing school as monotonous and boring and the teachers as overbearing pricks. That had the class in stitches. Brenda was laughing too, but she suggested it would be better if I didn't use profanity.

"Your writing is expressive. It's out there," Tammy praised.

"I wish I could write like you," I countered. Tammy's writing was so descriptive, it was as if she was drawing a picture. Her writing about her father's dying from heart disease was very moving, and it brought back memories for me of when my mom was dying.

She seemed like a very sweet girl, but the one black mark against her was that she was going out with one of the goons from the football team, Johnny Tommasulo. I had always wondered how Tammy could be involved with a hunk of shit such as Tommasulo. Tommasulo was a big kid, about 6-foot-2, and he never hesitated to throw his size and weight around. For reasons that only he could fathom, if he was even capable of thinking, he had picked me up and thrown me into a thorn bush on the side of the school property. This was back during my junior high school days.

Those thorns hurt, and I got all cut up. I never forgot that experience, and from that day onward, I had a negative opinion of the brainless twit.

When Tammy asked me if I wanted to join her for an after-school snack at the donut shop, I was hesitant.

"What about your boyfriend? Will he get pissed off at the both of us if he finds out?"

"I broke it off with him, Roddy," Tammy explained sadly. "I caught him kissing another girl, and I told him I never want to see him again."

We walked up to the Lane Diner on New Dorp Lane, one of Staten Island's main streets for shopping. After we ordered our coffees and donuts, Tammy started to break down at the table.

"I don't know what's wrong with me; I still love him," she sobbed.

"What?" I asked disbelievingly.

"I don't think it's Johnny's fault. He seems confused. He doesn't know what he wants. It's that new girl, Diane Annazulo. She's causing the trouble, and she knows I was going out with him."

"Confused? He's a dick for doing what he did to you. Forget he exists."

"No, you don't understand. He's really a sweet guy. Johnny is not himself lately."

Tammy was in denial. She was rationalizing the asshole's behavior. Now she wanted him back? Love makes people do stupid things, and this was one of them.

"All I know," I said, "is that I wish I had a girlfriend. A girlfriend like you who is so loyal, especially to the big bag of shit who calls himself a football player, and deserves far better than that."

"Wow, you really hate Johnny!" Tammy stated in amazement.

"He's a shithead," I explained. "Why would I like a person like that? Did you know that he tossed me into a thorn bush back in junior high, and you want me to think he's a sweet guy? A person like Tommasulo is a huge pile of shit!"

I realized I was being quite vulgar with Tammy, but I really didn't care. Why do nice girls like her always go for imbeciles like Tommasulo? Nice guys like myself couldn't get a glance, because we weren't "cool enough" for whatever perverse reason high school girls have.

Whenever a girl starts talking about her boyfriend as a real sweet guy, it's all bullshit. Chances are, she's going out with a parasite; and in Tommasulo's case, he was an overgrown slug. I had seen him slap a kid who was the same size as I was in front of his jock buddies. The kid whirled around to fight back, but when he realized Tommasulo's size, he backed down.

I wasn't finished with my rant yet, and I probably should have quit while I was ahead.

"Yeah, Tammy, Johnny's a really sweet guy, balling another girl behind your back. What consideration! Keep believing Johnny is so sweet and good, and maybe he'll come running back to you. And I have a bridge to sell you!"

"Stop!" Tammy wailed in protest. "Just shut up! You don't know what you're talking about! Johnny's a good guy. He really is!"

"Then why are you having a snack with me and not him?"

Tammy started crying uncontrollably, and I really could give a shit. Maybe I should have had more sympathy, but in this case, I couldn't understand pining over a dickweed.

A high school girl wailing over her boyfriend seemed so trivial to me at the time, especially in light of what I had gone through. The solution was really simple: "Get rid of him." I grabbed my coat and headed for the door.

On my way out, I noticed a gaggle of three bimbos staring at us through the window. They were looking at one another and squealing over the tale of idiotic gossip they would have for the next day.

I looked back at a still-sobbing Tammy, and I knew I had to say something to her that was a lot less harsh than I felt.

"Tammy, I'm sorry, but it's over. Move on." Her tears were tugging at my heart, just a little.

I exited the doorway and glared angrily at the three bimbos with their mile-high hair piled above them.

"If she's your friend, why don't you try helping her? She's upset about her boyfriend, and I can't help her. Do something useful with yourselves instead of gossiping like a pack of hens."

The bimbos stared at me, their mouths agape. I walked away from them and down New Dorp Lane back to Hylan Boulevard to catch the bus home.

As I suspected, even the good deed of having a snack with a jilted girl would come back to haunt me the next morning. Before classes started, students were herded like cattle into the cafeteria in order to wait. They didn't allow students up to their classes until 10 minutes before the start time of 8 a.m. Usually, I was never this early; I was just on time or late. The history teacher, Thorgensen, never seemed to mind, because I was acing his quizzes with 90 or above.

The cafeteria was packed and not an empty seat could be found. I was looking around for someone I would recognize, but someone who recognized me pushed me hard, knocking me onto the floor.

"Scumbag, what is this bullshit with my girlfriend?"

It was Johnny Tommasulo, snarling and snorting like the animal he was.

I had to act fast here. "Whoa, I don't know what you heard, but your girlfriend invited me to have coffee and donuts with her. She says she still loves you, but I can't figure out why. She was crying, and she was all upset about it. She really loves you, and you really hurt her, man."

That didn't soften his stance toward me. "Do me a favor. Mind your own fuckin' business, asshole." Having said that, he kicked me in the face, splitting open my lip. Enraged, I jumped on top of Tommasulo and I started pounding on his head, but my punches were mere mosquito bites that had no effect on him, and the big ape shook me off like a ragdoll.

Most kids in the cafeteria were half-asleep when I had arrived. By this time, the commotion had awakened them, providing them an adrenaline rush that was more effective than caffeine, and many were on their feet hollering and whooping up a storm, sort of the way they cheered on the then-popular ultra-right-wing Morton Downey Jr. show: "Woo, woo, woo, woo, woo!"

Before Tommasulo could advance after me, I pushed a nearby student off his chair. The chair was my equalizer, and I started swinging wildly at Tommasulo's hulking frame. I managed to connect with his left arm. Tommasulo instinctively grabbed his arm, and that gave me enough time to smack him in the head with the plastic chair. He buckled from the shot, and the students all let out a collective groan.

Before any further damage could be done, I was grabbed from behind by a security guard, a 20-something body-builder type named Tony.

"Let go of the chair; just let go of the chair," Tony urged.

I dropped the chair, and in the midst of the awakened morons — who acted as if they had never seen a fight before — I was escorted out of the cafeteria and into the dean's office.

This was my first visit to the dean's office. Dean Howard, a tall balding man with a no-nonsense face, was not amused by my roughhouse tactics.

"A chair? What were you thinking? You really could have hurt that kid."

I explained to the dean the whole story. What is a small person supposed to do against an oversized gorilla?

"Regardless," the dean said, "this is behavior we cannot condone. You're a senior, an upperclassman, and you're supposed to conduct yourself in a better fashion than that. We have underclassmen who are impressionable, and you seniors are the role models, the ones who have to set a good example."

I guess it was okay to have my head slapped around. "Why don't you say that to the asshole I was fighting with?"

"Don't worry, I'll take care of him. That will be my business. But as far as you are concerned, I'm suspending you for two days."

I was livid. "What kind of shit is this? This asshole knocks me to the ground, kicks me, and you're suspending me for defending myself? This is wrong and friggin' stupid."

Dean Howard was slowly brimming with anger. "I would advise you, Mr. McPherson, to keep your mouth shut. You're in enough trouble as it is. Don't turn bad into worse."

My aunt was called up to school, much to her chagrin. She glowered at me with anger when she arrived, but once she heard the full story her stance softened. Now she turned her anger against the dean.

"Yer suspending him for defending himself. I saw the size of the boy in that waiting room. He's huge like a mountain. True, that boy has an ice pack on his head, but what did you expect Roddy to do? Get his noggin taken off? My nephew has a good conduct record in this school. He's never been in trouble before. I'm sure there must have been times where kids picked on him and he never fought back, but now that he's finally getting some backbone, yer coming down hard on him!"

The dean was doing his utmost to placate my aunt. "Mrs. McPherson, I don't condone any kind of violence. I understand your nephew was defending himself, but using a chair is very extreme. That boy's neck could have been broken."

"And my nephew was kicked in the face by a size-13 foot! Will ye suspend that animal outside, or are ye going to slap him on his wrist?"

"Mrs. McPherson, they are both suspended. I can't allow violence in this school of any kind."

We exited the office. I saw Tommasulo nursing his head with an ice pack. We glared at each other, but no words were spoken as my aunt and I headed for home. She lectured me. "I know this is isn't yer fault, Roddy, but that goat of a dean doesn't understand that. For God sakes, try to stay out of trouble. Yer graduating in a few months, so stay away from girls who have just broken up with their boyfriends. Those two still carry torches for one another. Better to mind yer own business."

My mistake was going over to the diner with Tammy. I have enough problems in my life without being a counselor.

I spent the rest of that day watching TV, particularly the crappy *People's Court* with Judge Wapner and MTV with VJ Downtown Julie Brown, and all these hotties shaking their asses to the latest dance tunes at the New York Palladium. Metal head, big-haired Adam Curry followed Brown next with his hard-rock picks. The music scene was so lame, and how I wished they still had the 4:30 movie on Channel 7, WABC. That was a really special event for me when I would come home from school. I loved that intro with the cameraman plying his trade in the darkness with the fanfare music in the background. That special programming cultivated my love for the movies. *Ben Hur, Planet of the Apes, Dirty Harry, Spartacus* and *Godzilla* were some of the movies I saw in the 4:30 time slot.

Cable didn't arrive in Staten Island until January 1988.

While watching all of this and becoming suitably bored by the 60 channels of shit, I couldn't help but think about the day's events, and I knew for sure that it was those bimbos that had been gawking at Tammy and me through the window who spilled the beans on us. If only I could have taken a chair to *their* heads!

While I was watching Phil Donahue moralize about teen pregnancy during the late afternoon, a call came in from Brenda Moriarty.

"I heard about what happened," she said. "Is it true that you used a chair in that fight?"

I explained to Brenda how it all transpired and how I thought it was wrong that I should be suspended for this.

"It's only today and tomorrow. Just look at it as a mental health holiday."

"But I already had one with you," I protested.

"Go to a museum. Make the most of it. You're still educating yourself while you're off."

That was Brenda, always viewing matters in a positive light. Still, the incident left a bitter taste in my mouth, and I was being penalized for merely defending myself.

The Return

I didn't do anything for myself the next day. All I did was just mope around and watch TV. I couldn't help but dwell on that incident over and over again. I should have told that girl, "Thanks, but no thanks." As sweet and cute as a button as she was, I wasn't looking to go out with her, but it would have been nice to have a female friend closer to my age range. Brenda was a friend as much as a teacher could be, but she was 11 years older and I always feel you can never relate to an age group you're no longer part of. I couldn't relate to a 7-year-old at the time because I had progressed way beyond that at age 17. Cartoons and toys were no longer a part of my world. And I doubt Brenda could relate to a couple of fools fighting over some girl. But that woman tried to relate to me as best as she could. She was young at heart, and her light-hearted approach was always a great way to end the day.

It was no surprise that I would be asked questions by other students about the fight. Some dunderheads asked me if I was trying to make a move on Tommasulo' s girl. It wasn't even so. I wanted no part of that soap opera, although just by going to a lousy diner with her, a gaggle of bimbos decided to gossip about our meeting, incensing Tommasulo, who did his best to use my face for punting. I explained this to the lunchroom crew and even to Corsi, who remarked that I must be making up for lost time since I had always ducked confrontations. That was true. I hated confrontations, and I still do to this day, but I had no choice back then.

Corsi had a girl, and he was telling me about how he wasn't "getting any," how she refused to "put out." I found myself before the Tommasulo incident thinking it would be nice to have a girl-friend; but after that, I didn't want to get involved with anyone.

"I'm staying by myself. I don't love anybody, especially in this shithole. And you gotta watch what you do around here. There are spies all over the place. I cannot wait till I'm out of here, John; I just can't fuckin' wait!"

"You're better off not having a girlfriend," Corsi said. "She always wants to be taken someplace, and I never have the money. Last weekend, it was the movies, then she wanted to go out to the diner for a late-night snack. The movies are getting more expensive. Then the next day, she wants to be taken to the mall, where she expects me to spend more money on her. It's insane!"

I had no desire to be with anyone as Corsi was recounting his tale of woe. But it would have been nice to have someone of the opposite sex take an interest in me. We all have egos, and we all desire attention on some level.

The boys at the lunch table, Aquino, Castigelli and McMahon, were all describing what a dick Tommasulo was and how they were happy to see that headshot with the chair. They saw it all unfold before their eyes, and they thought I received a raw deal with the suspension.

I didn't see Tommasulo that day, but I did see Tammy, naturally, since she was in my creative writing class. I avoided eye contact with her.

There was one point where I heard her call my name, but I refused to take the bait. I was angry at her as well as her "boyfriend." Despite the assurances from Corsi and the lunchroom gang, I was still bristling with anger at this soap opera, and I spent most of the class time staring out the window, looking toward the NYC skyline. Brenda was having us read short stories from some boring anthology, and I was not in the frame of mind to care about what one person wrote back in the 19th century. Give me something I can relate to!

My lack of interest certainly wasn't lost on Brenda; and as she always does, she came up to me after class, sitting backward on the desk in front of me.

"Roddy, let it go. It happened and it's over. I know you're angry, but the person you're going to hurt the most is you if you keep letting that anger bubble inside."

"You believe me! It wasn't my fault, and it's so friggin' unfair."

Brenda smiled wistfully. "Life is not always fair, my dear. Let me tell you a story about unfairness. Are you interested?"

My ears perked up. "Yeah."

"You're not going to look out the window while I'm telling you this, are you?" she joked.

"No," I laughed.

"Okay, last semester, I was teaching at Thomas Jefferson High in Brooklyn. It's a very tough school in a tough neighborhood. I had been teaching English classes there ever since I graduated from college. I started out as a 'sub' first. Now, I'm a pretty tall girl and I can handle myself very well. I also studied kickboxing, so if any physical confrontation arose, I could handle it."

"So, you never had problems?" I asked.

Brenda shook her head. "Of course I did. When I first started as a sub, you wouldn't believe what I went through. The abuse toward me was verbal. You wouldn't believe some of the things these kids would say. A lot of the taunting was very suggestive and sexual, certainly not ready for primetime. But the more I stayed around, the more I wanted to win these kids over. I grew to view teaching there as a challenge. The students seemed to respect and trust me after a while. Many of these kids come from broken homes, and they have a lot of frustrations in their lives. They're skeptical of any outside help as if there was a catch. I spent six years in that school, and I never wanted to work anywhere else. I felt as if I was making a difference in kids' lives, especially if I turned them on to reading and writing. So I felt I really had a home there."

I was perplexed. "What does this have to do with me?"

"*Uno minuto,* hon. Patience! I'm getting to that! In one of my classes last semester, I had these two boys, Mario and Willis. They were such friends, almost to the point of being inseparable. But on this particular day, those two were not getting along. It turned out they were after the same girl, and neither of them wanted the other to have her. They came into class trying to take their seats. They managed to trip into one another, and a fight broke out just before I could get the lesson started. They were fighting by the windowsill, and I was playing referee doing my best to break it up. One of them slugged me hard on my nose, breaking it. While I fell to the ground injured, Mario had Willis hanging out the window. The girls were screaming in the class, 'No!' I think Mario wanted to scare Willis by dangling him out of the window. He didn't want to hurt him. But he lost his grip on him, and Willis fell three stories to his death. This happened before I could get my wits about me."

I remembered reading a story in the *Staten Island Advance* last year about two kids fighting in an inner-city neighborhood school and one of them falling out of a window during the struggle. I hadn't realized that Brenda had a major role in this story.

She continued: "Willis's parents were really grief-stricken, and they were not only angry at Mario but with me as well, feeling I could have stopped the fight. I remembered attending the funeral and paying my condolences to Willis's mother. She slapped me hard across the face and said, 'It's your fault my baby's dead, you incompetent bitch. You could have saved my baby, but you didn't.'"

Brenda started to choke back tears as she continued. "There was an inquiry into the matter by the Board of Ed., and my broken nose was evidence enough to exonerate me from any wrongdoing. But the school decided to give me a leave of absence. They also felt it was best that I get transferred somewhere else."

"I'm sorry," I murmured. "That wasn't fair, and it wasn't your fault."

"That's my point," Brenda stated. "There are circumstances in life that do occur, and life is not always fair. You were suspended, but at least you're back in school."

"Whatever happened to Mario?"

"Mario is serving time at a juvenile facility," she answered grimly. "That poor kid must be going through hell. I could tell when Willis fell to his death that Mario never wanted to do that to Willis. He was shocked most of all that it happened. I visited him back in December and he looked gaunt, defeated. God knows the abuse he's suffering up there."

"And you forgave him for breaking your nose?"

"It was a heat-of-the-moment impulse, Roddy. I tried to break up the fight, and this what happens when you play referee."

She paused thoughtfully for a moment and added, "I really believe there is no such thing as a bad kid. If you can reach kids, you can help them a great deal, and they are no worse than adults. I just wish I could have helped Mario and Willis more."

Talk about unfair. But Thomas Jefferson High's loss was Normand High's gain. What I really liked about Brenda was that she didn't talk down to me like other teachers or authority figures did.

Speaking of hard-assed teachers, my typing skills were still atrocious, much to the dismay of Mrs. Welsh. She once again was walking around the room with her black book, looking for any infractions.

"McPherson, stop looking at the keyboard. You're a very nice young man, but you always make mistakes. You always have to cheat!"

I didn't get offended or insulted. It was humorous to me. I was a lousy typist, but it wasn't a course that was required for graduation.

Cool and Hip

I was something of a celebrity upon my return to the Record Den. The punks who would normally say hi and shuffle on to their record browsing were engaging me in lengthy conversation. We had never talked before because we had nothing in common.

This one particular kid, Kent, who sported a multicolored mohawk, was quizzing me about the holdup.

"Holy shit! That is so awesome!" Kent said. "I mean, I would have been shitting bricks if that was me."

Meanwhile, Erika extended another invitation to me. "Roddy, why don't you come over to the Bowery Ballroom tonight? My band has another gig."

I appreciated Erika's overtures, but I just didn't belong with the punk crowd. It was a style of music I didn't care for and I, a kid with long hair parted in the middle, would not fit in whatsoever with the mohawked crowd.

"I don't think so, Erika, but thanks anyway." Truth be told, I was still depressed over Tammy and Tommasulo. I wasn't in the mood for company.

"Oh, c'mon, Roddy, what's the excuse this week?" Erika demanded.

I told her about the incident with Tommasulo and his girl. "You can't help anyone," I decided.

"I appreciated your help that day," Erika stated. "My life passed before my eyes. There were bullets in that nutjob's gun. I was never so scared, and I never thanked you properly for it."

She gave me a hug. "Please come to the club," she pleaded. "It would mean so much to me. You're a friend."

I went. What else did I have to do, and I needed to get out of the funk I was in.

The club was an old-style theater that had seen better days. The seats had been taken out ages ago, and there was a bar by the entrance, which is where I stayed. I didn't want any part of the stage, which was crammed with multicolored hair and mohawked punks pogoing and slam-dancing into one another. And I always hated being hemmed in. What if there was a fire? You would be as good as dead, because you would be crushed during the ensuing panic.

I sat at the bar, downing Budweiser, watching the spectacle unfold before me. The sound was the usual punk sludge I had become accustomed to and had grown to hate when going to Killian's gigs or listening to the records at the shop that Erika had insisted on playing. As far as the singing went, Erika was reduced to shrill screaming. It was good for what it was, I guess, but I will give Erika this: she was definitely animated and entertaining.

After the fourth song, I had more than enough and I was ready to vacate the premises — until Erika made a special announcement.

"I want to bring on a special friend tonight. Some of you may know I work at the Record Den on East 8th Street. I was involved in a holdup last week until my co-worker and friend stopped this guy who had a gun on me. I want you all to meet him. He's my hero. Please welcome, Roddy McPherson! Get your ass up here on stage, Roddy! Whooooooo!"

It was both embarrassing and exhilarating. Embarrassing, because I never like to make a fuss about myself. Exhilarating, because it was so stirring to have people cheer and shout out your name. It was nice to be lauded as a hero, and truth be told, I needed this lift after the lousy week I had.

Some of the punks tried to engage me in conversation, but it was hard to hear over the wall of noise that was Erika's music. It was ironic, because when I first arrived, the multicolored and mohawked brigade looked upon me as in "Who the fuck is this?"

I soon exited the place. It just wasn't my scene.

And the Hits Keep Coming

Just because I was hailed as a hero in some quarters didn't mean everyone took to me. Tommasulo certainly didn't. I learned a basic tenet, which was, "Not everyone is going to like you in life."

The month of March was coming to a close, and I was happy about that. Despite warm waves, spring hadn't settled in yet and I was looking forward to the opportunity to sit outside in beautiful Von Briesen Park.

The passing of time meant that my days at Normand High were numbered. I would be launched into the adult world. All I had to do was keep my record clean as far as behavior was concerned.

Staying clean was a lot harder in practice than theory. During my weight-training class on one of those late March spring days, this oversized King Guido shit named Doug snapped a towel in my face. He struck me just above my left eye, where I had gotten butted with a rifle from one of the bank robbers. The sensation of pain was stinging. In anger, I kicked Doug's knee hard in retaliation, hoping to dislocate it.

"Oww, mother fucker!" the guido yelped while clutching his knee. He snapped the towel at me some more. I managed to grab a hold of it, determined to wrest it away from him.

"Whatsamatter, you can't take a joke? What's your problem?"

"You, asshole, are my problem. How would you like it if I snapped the towel at you?" I loosened the grip on the towel and procured a Swiss army knife out of my gym shorts pocket.

I had the blade opened and it gleamed off the gymnasium's lights.

"Do that again," I warned, "and I'll take your fuckin' eye out."

Doug was looking at me disbelievingly and was no longer the cocky, abusive guido. "All right, buddy, take it easy. You're fuckin' nuts!"

I really would have liked to strangle the sonuvabitch with that towel. I know that in a test of strength with the goon, I would have lost, which is why I whipped out the knife.

Racial Conflict

I started carrying the knife after the holdup. It made me feel much more secure, and threatening Doug was the first time I had ever made some use of it. But I wondered if I would actually use the damn thing. Uncle Tim had purchased it for me two Christmas seasons ago, but it just lay in my room, buried in a bureau drawer, more so as a collection piece; but I was now depending on it as a weapon of self-defense.

Would I have hurt Doug? I wasn't setting out to, but if he tried to hurt me further, I would have no choice but to defend myself with the knife. I would have been wiped off the floor in a physical fight with him. I only got lucky with Tommasulo; if there were no chair, my head would have been taken off.

Tommasulo, as his want, got involved in a fracas with Steve Eder. The action unfolded on one of the specialized city buses the school utilized to take students. There was no more beef between Tommasulo and myself; the dean made us promise him that we would have no contact with each other whatsoever. And I think I proved to him I had no interest in his girl, who was still in love with him. I questioned her intelligence, but I was naive in love relationships.

Steve was already seated by the time that lumbering lummox came onto the bus, and as Tommasulo passed Steve, he slapped him across the head. Steve took umbrage, jumped on top of his seat and managed to smack Tommasulo on the back of the head with his loose-leaf book. Tommasulo turned back toward Steve and punched him so hard in the face, he tumbled out of his seat. Before Tommasulo could advance any further on his prey, Steve pulled out a blade and stabbed him in the left thigh. Tommasulo started freaking out from the blood and pain: "Oh, shit! He stabbed me; the little nigger stabbed me!" I don't think Tommasulo ever expected that, and neither did the other students. Everyone stood up and gathered around the pair. The bus driver, an elderly man, had heard all the ruckus and pushed his way toward the back of the bus.

"Goddamnit, what the hell is going on back here? Another fight?" Then he saw Tommasulo holding his bloodied leg and Steve holding the bloodied knife. "Oh my God!"

The bus driver motioned to Steve very calmly. "Son, just give me the knife, please."

Steve seemed most surprised at all that he had stabbed Tommasulo. I truly believe he didn't mean to. But he snapped. He handed the knife over limply to the bus driver.

The bus driver regained his composure and started barking orders: "Everybody, off the goddamn bus, now! Move! But nobody go anywhere. We'll need witnesses. Let me radio for some goddamn help! Jesus Christ, what a mess!"

The driver radioed his dispatch, and within minutes, a police car and ambulance arrived. I slinked away from the scene, and looking back on it, perhaps I should have stuck around to give my version of the events, and to add some support for Steve. I simply didn't wish to get involved.

Of course, the newspapers would report it the next day. But the media, as always, fucked it up, claiming that this was a racial incident. It was not a racial incident. In all fairness to Tommasulo, there was nothing racial about what he did. He was an equal-opportunity prick who loved bullying around kids shorter than himself. He had received his comeuppance as far as I was concerned.

There was an assembly that day with Principal DiMartino, who lectured the students about racism and violence, and how these wanton acts would not be tolerated. I shook my head in disgust.

Tammy Brascia wasn't in school that day. No doubt, she was nursing that dipshit's wounds. And Brenda decided to have us write down our feelings about the incident. Most in the class condemned the violence, expressing annoyance and shock that Steve could commit such a horrible act. I was one of only two people who supported Steve, writing that it was absolutely justified. Steve was merely defending himself, and would people have preferred that he'd have his head taken off by Tommasulo? I also wrote that Tommasulo was the biggest jerkoff in the school and that if two people had issues with him, the blame didn't lie with them. I also expressed regret that I didn't stick around to defend Steve. Maybe it wouldn't have made a difference, because once Steve pulled that knife, he was a goner.

Latiesha Wilkins, a black girl in the class, knew Steve, and agreed with me. She wasn't sure if there was racism involved, but she said she wouldn't have been surprised. Then she threw this statement out to the class: "A 6-foot-2 kid is slapping the head of another kid half his size. What did you expect him to do?"

Brenda sat back on her desk and took it all in. Her opinion was that while she didn't condone Steve bringing along a knife, she did understand why he did what he had to. "It's not the first time he's probably been picked on, and he was being picked on because of his size. Whether racism was involved, I don't know, but Roddy has had trouble with this particular boy. And he stated that other kids have too."

It was gutsy of Brenda to have the class write about that topic, and it was an important one. No matter what your feelings were on the matter, it was definitely a provocative topic, and it really got the creative juices of everyone in the class stirred.

Brenda talked to Latiesha and me after the class. She commended us for our perspective and for speaking our minds.

"I'm thinking of starting a writing workshop after school," she announced. "I'm not sure when it will be, but I would really like to have it. I would want you two to be involved. Would you be interested?"

We definitely wanted to be involved, and Brenda was going to try and get something going with the English Department head. However, the following day, Brenda told us it was a no-go with the department. And she received a verbal warning from the department head that if she ever tried to talk about a controversial subject again in class such as the Steve-Tommasulo subject, she would be terminated.

"That stinks," I said. "How did the department head know?"

Brenda shrugged and smiled. "Someone from the class told her. I don't know who, but you know how high school kids gossip."

"It certainly wasn't us," Latiesha affirmed. "We need to talk about things like that instead of sweeping it under the rug."

"It was the best topic yet," I decided.

"Thanks, you two. Now, I'm not allowed to hold a writing workshop here, but I might be able to hold one privately. I have to see what I can do with my schedule."

The Nightmares Persist

I couldn't sleep without a nightlight. Those dark-clothed figures stood in my hallway, and I passed right through them. Even though they were just a figment of my imagination, they were all too real, and I didn't want to see them again.

I was always looking over my shoulder and I became quite jumpy, even when someone just called my name. Even Brenda had to say, "Relax, hon" at one point.

And when someone was walking behind me, I kept turning my head back. It was just not a normal way of living. When was the next person going to jump me? Would I get mugged and beaten up again?

The nightmares had made so paranoid, I felt I needed a gun. Those muggings and robberies were traumatic experiences. I wouldn't have wished them on anyone at the time except for Tommasulo, but he had paid his price.

I watched the movie *Death Wish,* and marveled at how it would be great if I could plug a few of the skells that tried to mess with me. The idea stuck in my craw, but could I really obtain a gun in NYC? I didn't even know which illegal channels I could go through.

I bought a Guns Deluxe magazine at a nearby candy store. The owner of the store gave me a raised eyebrow. Did he really think I was going to purchase a gun? Some people are truly ignorant. It was illegal to own one, and this was pure fantasy for me — a fantasy in which I could pull the trigger at the bad guys. A fantasy in which they got injured instead of me, or possibly killed. I used to have some sympathy for muggers, believing the bad conditions they endure in the slum neighborhoods would drive a man to do that, but it all seemed rather extreme after I went through my ordeals. You would have to be a person without caring, without feeling, without soul in order to brutalize a person. There is no moral justification for it.

I saw an advertisement for "prop" guns. Those were the kind they used on Hollywood sets. I had no intention of killing anyone, but I was not willing to be part of the maimed or the killed. But even that idea was knocked out of the box when a credit card or check was required for purchase. At that age, I had neither.

So I simply took the magazine and dumped it into the wastebasket. It had been a nice fantasy that lasted for all of two minutes.

Getting to Know Erika Better

"There's my buddy," Erika crowed as I came into the shop on a rainy Saturday morning. "You didn't stick around for the concert last week. Why?"

"Erika, it's not my scene," I replied.

"You could have stayed and had more fun. You are too serious sometimes, Roddy."

I knew that, but I couldn't relax as of late. Life had become so serious for me. There was this pressure of having a definitive idea of what I should be doing after high school. I didn't have a clue as to what I wanted to do, except film school. I wanted a creative career and not a humdrum 9-to-5 life. But would my aunt be willing to pay for that? And my lust for girls was starting to come into its peak at this stage. I wondered what it would be like to have a girlfriend and get laid.

"Well, what did you think of my band?" Erika asked.

"Oh, different. It was entertaining. I never knew you could scream like that."

Erika laughed. "You never saw me in an argument with my parents."

"How long have you been playing in a band?" I asked.

"Six months."

"I never knew that."

"You never ask anything about me," she complained. "You're so quiet. I have to make conversation with you."

"Wait a minute, I talk," I protested.

"Only if people say anything to you. When you come in here, you never even say hi!"

"I'm not good at greetings."

"It's me — Erika. I'm your friend."

"I never thought of you as a friend," I said simply.

Erika looked pained. "Why?"

"Because you're my co-worker! We never did anything together until last weekend. And I never saw you at the shop so much until two months ago. You were always on Sundays."

"That's true," but we're friends now."

"But you never seemed to be interested in me."

"Because you shut yourself away from everyone, Roddy. Even Rob says you're not an easy person to know. Not everyone you meet is out for something or looking to hurt you."

I let my guard down a bit. "I don't feel comfortable with people, Erika. I've been hurt a lot."

"You would never have to be afraid of me."

"To tell you the truth, I felt intimidated by you," I ventured.

"Why would you feel that?"

"Because you dress up in that punk getup, but it's stylish. I've never been stylish," I said, pointing out the Army jacket, flannel and jeans I had on. "And who would want a scrub like me for a friend?"

"A lot of people," Erika pointed out, "especially after what you did two weeks ago. But you're really a sweet person aside from that."

"But you're cool," I protested. "I never have been. I'm always the kid who was a punching bag until recently. People hated me."

"And those are jerks, Roddy. Why waste your opinion on them?"

She had a point. We got to know each other a lot better that day.

Erika aspired to be a clothing designer, attending the Fashion Institute of New York. She took out a sketch book of her designs, and they seemed very tasteful. I'm not a fashion expert, but I liked what I saw in those sketch books better than the clothing I had seen on news reports covering fashion shows. I'm talking about fashion so overblown, you would see it only on TV or at those exclusive fashion shows.

"You can find a lot of bargains on the Lower East Side," she commented, pointing to her low-cut top, her multicolored scarf and her cap.

"Why don't you come out with me for dinner?" she asked. "I have nothing planned tonight."

"What about your boyfriend, Mark?"

"What about him?" Mark was a tall, lanky kid who looked more nerdish than punkish, with black horn-rimmed glasses and spiked hair. But he seemed like a nice guy the few times I had seen him.

"He's hanging out with his buddies. He has his own life, and I have mine."

"No, I don't think it's a good idea," I answered.

"Roddy, don't be afraid. Mark is not like those super jocks from Staten Island. He has female friends too, and it doesn't bother me."

I was suspicious. "I find that hard to believe."

"Look, if he was seeing another girl weekend after weekend, I'd be concerned. But people in Manhattan are more open and not as uptight as they are in Staten Island. You have that whole macho he-man caveman subculture. Just because a guy and a girl have dinner doesn't mean they are going to have a love relationship."

We went off to an old-time Jewish deli on the Lower East Side called Katz's, which specialized in the most colossal sandwiches I have ever seen. Their corn beef and pastrami sandwiches were out of this world, and so were their "Coney Island fries," which Erika and I could barely finish.

"What are your plans after school, Roddy?"

"I want to become a street bum, eating out of trash cans," I joked.

"Cut it out. What are your plans?"

"I want to be a garbage man. I always wanted to smell orange juice and mowed-up grass baking in the sun. It's beautiful."

Erika was laughing. "Will you be serious for one moment?"

"What, I am serious! It's good money."

"Quit playing around!"

"Erika, I want to go into film. I want to write screenplays. But I'm better off being a garbage man because the competition is too stiff."

"If you really put your mind to it, I'm sure you would do really well. NYU has a great film program. Why don't you look into that?"

"I don't think my aunt can afford it; and even if she could, she wouldn't approve."

"You have to convince her it's what you really want to do. Do you really write screenplays?"

"I have tried, but it's hard. I've been taking a creative writing class, and I'm writing a lot."

"That's really cool. Is it a school course or an outside course?"

"It's a school class, but the teacher is really nice."

"I took a creative writing class in Brooklyn. It was run by a really cool teacher, Brenda Moriarty."

"Holy cow," I said in surprise. "She's my teacher!"

"That is so hysterical!" Erika said. "She's tall, redheaded. Her hairstyle is really huge."

I was confused. "She must have cut it, because it's short and spiky on top, long in the back."

"Wow. She must have. I swear to God, she looked like one of those metal chicks you see hanging out in L.A."

"She looks out for me," I stated, not really caring about what Brenda had looked like in the past, although that mental picture of her seemed rather intriguing. "Did you know she found me the day I was mugged? And after almost every class, she tries to talk to me."

"She really likes you," Erika added. "She did that me with me too. Brenda always thought I was preoccupied with death, but I wasn't. It's just that I found it easier to write about dark things. Dark things are more interesting to write about anyway, don't you think?"

I was afraid of death and dying, and I told Erika so.

"But it is inevitable, Roddy, don't you think? We all are going to die someday, and I'm prepared, probably more than most people."

This was a disturbing turn in the conversation, and I just shook my head.

"Why are you shaking your head, Roddy? For all we know, life after death may be bliss."

"I want to live my life," I said. "I don't want to know about death yet. I want to leave my mark in this world."

"And how is that?"

I finally had the answer: "By writing. Thanks to Brenda, I now know what path to take in life."

We walked about Manhattan a bit. We were both tired and not really wanting to do anything. She had been out the night before partying until 3 a.m. and was wanting to go home to Bay Ridge. I offered to take the R subway train with her, then I would catch the No. 79 bus that would take me to Staten Island. All I had to do was walk a few blocks to the bus stop from the subway station.

"How do you like living in Bay Ridge?" I asked Erika during the long train ride to the last outpost, 95th Street.

"It's okay, but Manhattan is so much better. It's where the action is. Brooklyn is still better than Staten Island. At least we have better bars and clubs. But the rock scene is dead here, and all we have is L'Amour's. You have to go to Manhattan for really good clubs."

There was a bit of silence afterward. We were exhausted. She asked about my plans for the upcoming Easter vacation.

"I have relatives up in the Catskills. My aunt and I are going up there for a few days."

"That's nice. I'm going out to L.A. with Mark. I never have been to California before."

Now that sounded a hell of a lot better than the Catskills. Hollywood, movie stars, the film industry. That was all up my ally. "Can I come too?" I joked.

"I wish I could take you," she said.

We bid our goodbyes as we got off the subway at 95th Street and 4th Avenue. I headed to my bus stop on 92nd Street while Erika headed to her apartment overlooking the Narrows on Shore Road.

The weather was cool that night, and as I zipped my jacket to my neck I wondered about Erika's remark about wishing she could take me to L.A. Was she really unhappy with her boyfriend? I did like her a lot despite her preoccupation with death that night. That was the only black mark against her.

Trip to the Country

My Uncle Ray's father used to be a farmer, which is why there was so much land around his house. I'd say there were 160 acres of land, including woods in the back. This was definitely a change from the city streets, and I needed the break from urban life.

Uncle Ray was a New York State Trooper, and Aunt Carol was an insurance adjustor. They had a 20-year-old daughter, Becky, who was attending the University of Binghamton further upstate in New York, majoring in sports medicine. So their lives were a comfortable middle-class existence. My aunt and uncle were both anti-New York City. "That city is such a sewer," my Aunt Carol remarked. "Why don't you move out of there, Jane?"

"The police are not allowed to do their jobs down there," Uncle Ray weighed in. "They're too liberal, which is why you have victims like Roddy. They have to take names and kick ass. You can't be humane with these criminals."

I asked Uncle Ray about gun control and his position on it.

"Only the police and military should be allowed to carry firearms. I have seen the result of too many accidents with guns."

He had a point, but then again, he had never been mugged on the streets. He was a law enforcement officer who had the right to carry a gun. What about an ordinary citizen, such as me, who needed to protect himself? "What do people like Aunt Jane and myself do?" I asked.

"You move," Uncle Ray declared. "You move to the suburbs or the country."

"It's not so simple," Aunt Jane replied. "My job is there, and you can't get a job so easily nowadays."

I wondered if I could ever be happy living in the country. As serene as this living was, it could get boring. What do you do for culture, entertainment, the arts and sports? While living on Staten Island, I could hop aboard a bus, ferry or train, and I would be transported to the nerve center of the city, Manhattan.

Where else could you go see works like those in the Guggenheim or the Museum of Modern Art? In those places, you had paintings in which it looked like dogs had dipped their paws in paint and walked all over the canvases. I admired that art, as crazy as it seemed. Who would have thought there would be a market for Andy Warhol and his paintings of Campbell's soup cans, but there was and the man was a genius. Pop art is good fun, and art is something you shouldn't have to analyze.

Cousin Becky saved me from boredom. If it wasn't for her, I would have certainly been picking dirt out of my toenails. "What do you folks do up here?" I asked, not unreasonably.

"There is plenty to do up here. You have to have wheels."

She took me places, such as Howe Caverns, which was really unique in the fact that you boarded a boat in the midst of water inside the cave. And the town of Woodstock was very hippie/yuppie oriented. That Woodstock nation bull is such a crock. Most of them were so stoned, they didn't even know they were starving in the mud, while listening to music performed by musicians so far away, they might as well have been ants. The exceptions were the audience members closest to the stage. And the sound speakers were really shitty at the time, so how could this have been a good experience? Peace and love. These zombies could have cared less about political change. All they cared about was getting stoned, listening to music if they could hear it and getting laid. The intentions of the hippie love generation were noble, and wouldn't it be great to have worldwide peace? I would have loved peace back in my senior year, but let's be honest here as to what Woodstock was all about.

I told Becky this theory when I was able to loosen up, and she laughed at me. "You are so cynical living in that city. I don't think it's as bad as my father makes it to be. I want to come down there in the summer. I hope my parents let me stay with you and Aunt Jane."

Another fun activity we did one day was take target practice with a pistol: a .25 automatic. Uncle Ray took it upon himself to teach me firearm safety. The pistol was simple to use. The kickback was slight, but still not easy to get used to right away. By the end of the day, I was hitting the targets dead center.

It was good therapy for me to hit those targets in that large back yard. And while taking target practice, I took in the sheer expanse of the land. I was a novice to real estate, but I commented to Becky that they could get a lot of money for this land.

"I don't think we'll ever leave this land," she commented. "It's home to us. That would be like cutting off our arms."

The scenery in the upstate was breathtaking with the rolling inclines of farmland, and I felt really safe up there. My New York City anxieties and fears melted away in the town of East Durham.

"What do you plan to do after school is over?" Becky asked.

"I'm thinking of film school, but I don't know if my aunt will pay for it."

"Are you sure that's what you want to do with your life?"

Who could ever be sure at that age of what you really wanted. I was basically talentless, but I liked film and I had finished a rough screenplay draft of a vigilante movie, which no one knew about, with the exception of Killian. My aunt had given me a camcorder for Christmas, but I hardly used it. I had brought it with me on this trip to film some scenery, but I felt rather odd just taking it out and filming people. Would my Aunt Carol and Uncle Ray be tolerant of me running around with a camcorder? I doubt it.

"You should use your camera. If I know anything about the film field, you can't be shy. You have to be more assertive and more outgoing," Becky encouraged.

"I guess I can film you shooting off your gun," I suggested.

"Hell, why not?" Becky said with a laugh.

Becky was the all-American girl type; curly-haired, freckle-faced, apple-cheeked skin. She was cute, and her personality was kind and considerate. Becky was athletic, starring as a pitcher for her college softball team. Where I was quiet and withdrawn, she was gregarious and outgoing. I found it odd that she wanted to spend time with her boring cousin, but she was a gracious host.

"You're family, Roddy. I never get to see you."

"This is not a boring vacation for you?"

"It's a pleasure to come back home from college. Sometimes there is too much partying at the dorm. Letting your hair down is good, but a lot of kids I know abuse alcohol really badly. They have drinking problems, and it's sad to see. Very sad."

"Don't you have friends?"

"Sure, I do, but they are mostly my dorm mates, and I could use the quiet. Like I said, the partying is fun at times, but it can get out of hand." After a pause, she added, "I'm glad to be home, very glad. I never thought I'd miss home, but I do."

I took film footage of Becky shooting pistols, clowning about, and she in turn took footage of me firing the pistols as well. As sick as this sounds, I enjoyed firing that .25. It was good therapy, and I was surprised at how good my aim really was.

It was with great sadness that I left the Catskills to come back to Staten Island. And I really enjoyed spending time with cousin Becky. How many girls do you know who are into firing pistols? In liberal New York City, she would be frowned upon as a gun nut, but I found her charming, down to earth and a lot nicer than most of the girls I was going to school with.

The Beginning of the Final Stretch

The weather started to warm up a little after I returned back to school. Up in the Catskills, it was cold, never getting above 50 degrees. In Staten Island, we were seeing temps in the 60s, which is my kind of weather.

I was counting the days until my exit out of high school. It still didn't feel real that I would be graduating, but it was just two months away. In the meantime, I muddled through most of my classes but relished Brenda's. She asked the students to write about their favorite vacation spot. I chose California, a place I had never been to yet but hoped to. The Mediterranean temperatures and constant sunshine made it seem ideal. Perhaps I would settle out there and become an actor.

Brenda laughed at my suggestion. "Somehow, Roddy, I don't think you're the acting type. You would be best suited as a screenwriter."

The woman had me pegged, but I would love to play the *Dirty Harry* role that Eastwood made famous. Especially in light of what had happened to me, I found the theme of suppressing crime and dishing out law and order very appealing. I guess I could become a cop. But it's never like the movies, perhaps worse. How could I deal with maggots, filth and the scumbags of society? In less than three months, I had more than my fill.

I saw Brenda after class, and I chided her that she killed my dream.

"Face it sweetie, I'm saving you heartbreak and rejection."

"But I do love screenwriting. As a matter of fact, I'm working on one right now."

"Oh, really?" Brenda perked up with interest. "Why didn't you ever say anything to me about that?"

"You might think it's stupid," I reasoned.

"Writing is never stupid, Roddy. What's your screenplay about?"

"A kid turns vigilante."

Brenda chuckled. "I certainly don't have to ask where you got the inspiration, but movies like *Death Wish* have been done to death. I will admit that having a kid vigilante is quite unique."

"I also want to make films," I added. "While I was up in the Catskills, I was messing around with my camcorder. I liked that experience of filming things."

"If it's something you really want to do, then go for it," Brenda urged. "But make sure it's what you want first. It's a very tough industry to crack. Make sure you are dedicated to your craft."

"It may never work out. My aunt wouldn't support this. I don't think she has the money for me to attend film school."

"You're a good writer; why not become a journalist or reporter?"

I tasted the suggestion unhappily. "I can't see myself as a reporter."

"You would grow into it," Brenda reasoned. "And you seem to have a natural bent for writing. Nothing else seems to interest you. It would probably be better for you than going into the film industry. There's a lot of competition, especially with screenplays. If you think publishing a novel is tough, getting a screenplay accepted by the studio is tougher. Many screenplays are written and submitted to studios, but few are ever made into movies. Look at the ratio of movies compared to books."

If I hadn't come off my Catskill high by the beginning of the school week, my conversation with Brenda was certainly doing the trick. "You are depressing me," I protested.

"I'm trying to help you, Roddy. Be realistic. But it's your life, and you have to make that call yourself. If screenwriting is what you really want to do, be prepared to struggle."

I knew Brenda had my best interests at heart. So did my aunt. But unlike my aunt, Brenda wasn't chiding and scolding me about my future. She was offering suggestions and alternatives.

Before I left the room, I asked Brenda about Erika.

"Oh, yeah, the punkette," she said, laughing. "She really is a sweet girl and a good writer of poetry. But she was very dark in her writings and always preoccupied with death and dying. I found it a little disconcerting."

"Did you ask her about it?"

"She said it was just an interest. She wasn't going to jump off any buildings, and she had no intentions of dying. It was her favorite subject, but I reminded her that perhaps she should explore topics a lot less morbid."

"I was with her a couple of weekends. We ate out together, and she was going on about how we shouldn't be afraid of death. It was a little creepy. I like Erika, but the conversation was too deep."

"I'm not a psychologist," Brenda stated, "but it makes you wonder if she truly has a death trip. If you do see her, tell her I said hi."

The Need to Feel Safe

If Erika had a secret death wish, she could have it to herself. I wanted to live for as long as I could. I had cheated death twice and had no intentions of engaging in that dance so soon.

I called Rob to tell him I would be running late. "No big deal. Erika is there." As much as I liked Erika, I was beginning to get a bit put out by her always being there on Saturdays. I was supposed to be the Saturday clerk. If Rob was so fearful about his business losing money, he should just let Erika work Sundays, as she was supposed to. I was hired strictly for Saturdays.

Regardless, I didn't mind Erika covering for me on that particular day. I had to attend to some serious business. While up in the Catskills, I had loved the feeling of carrying that pistol Becky had let me use for target practice. And I still felt ill at ease walking around the city. I realized it was important to get out of the house and work, but I was always fearful of getting jumped again. If I thought enough about the beating, I could still feel the kicks and punches raining down on me.

I was still a kid, not yet 18 years old and not yet an adult, yet here I was scared and jittery like the old people back in that Highbridge neighborhood in the Bronx. I needed a "tool" to keep me safe.

There was a gun shop on the Bowery. I walked inside, and a tough-looking, burly guy behind the counter eyed me suspiciously. "Uh, hi," I began nervously. "I'd like to buy a gun."

The gun shop owner looked me over. "Are you serious?"

"I am. If I don't get a gun, I won't make it out there on the streets. I'm going to get killed."

"Look, kid, you have to have a license to buy a gun. You know guns are illegal in the city, so why are you wasting my time and yours?"

I was lost for words. "I, uh, ahh, fuck it!" I turned to exit out the door.

"Wait a minute!" the gun shop owner barked. "I know you. You're that kid who stopped that crack addict in a record store a month ago, right? And you were also mugged on Staten Island in St. George, right?"

"Yeah, you read about me?"

He softened a bit. "I live on Staten Island myself, in New Dorp. I read all about you. You disarmed that guy in that record shop. What do you need a gun for?"

That was a stupid question to ask. "I'm not Superman," I blurted out.

"Come into the back room with me," he instructed.

We went into his stockroom, which was very tight and narrow. Out of the many random boxes he had on the shelf, the owner produced a .9 millimeter handgun. The shop owner looked at me intently. "Have you ever shot a gun?"

"Yes," I answered. "A .25 automatic. I have a cousin up in the Catskills, and she taught me how to take target practice with one."

The shop owner did a double take. "She? You don't get too many girls who are into guns."

"Well, this girl is."

"Look, I can't sell you a handgun. Both of us could get into serious trouble. This is a replica of a .9 millimeter. All this does is fire blanks. You don't ever want to find yourself shooting at anyone. You just want to be able to scare people away if they try to mess with you."

I wasn't in any position to argue. "I'll take it. I really don't care."

"This will cost you about 100 dollars."

"Sold," I simply said.

"All right," the man said as he placed it in a bag for me. "I shouldn't be doing this, and I could get into trouble even by selling you this. As far as I'm concerned, this conversation never took place. I don't know you and you don't know me."

I nodded again as I handed him over the bills.

"Now get the hell out of here, and like I said, this exchange never happened."

"I got ya, and thanks." I proceeded to walk out of the store.

I reached the record shop about 11 in the morning, but not before I got myself a bagel and coffee. I kept the gun and cartridges inside my jacket pocket. Already I felt invincible. It's amazing how much a small weapon can boost your confidence.

Now no one will be able to fuck with me, I thought.

Gay and Homeless Issues

Rob and Erika's activity for the day was to put down Staten Island, as if it were such a horrible place. They felt it was nowhere, the people living on the Island were backwards, and they felt so sorry for me.

"There are things to do on Staten Island," I protested. "There's Bay Street."

"Big deal," Erika snorted. "Those clubs suck. In Brooklyn, we have L'Amours."

"Yeah, man," Rob chimed in. "If Staten Island is so good, why do you come here to work? Don't you have any record stores over there? You live in a one-horse town."

I looked at Rob as if he was an idiot, which sometimes he really was. "Yeah, there are record shops. It's just that they weren't hiring. And the Island is not a one-horse town. It's quite developed. How would you know anything about it? You can't even remember Woodstock."

My rejoinder to Rob cracked Erika up. She enjoyed instigating this whole conversation, proclaiming Staten Island as dullsville.

I thought I would have the final say on the matter when I cited the crime statistics of Staten Island versus Manhattan.

"Oh, yeah?" Erika shot back. "Where did you get mugged? Where did you get smacked in the head with a gun? Staten Island is so much safer?"

It was no good arguing. Staten Island was safer than Manhattan. The statistics bore that out. But I had more criminal incidents happen to me on the Island compared with Manhattan. One mugging and one store robbery on Staten Island compared with one store robbery in Manhattan. Statistically speaking, I was safer in Manhattan, but not by much.

"I'm going to the store," I announced to Erika and Rob, who were chortling with glee. "I'll be back in a few."

"Aw, come on back, Roddy," Erika called from behind me. "You're so easy to tease. And fun too."

I did enjoy the teasing too. Like I had said before, it was my home away from home. I could count my friends on my fingers only. Erika and Rob were two of them.

Erika was going on about how she was going to revolutionize fashion, and how it was so boring with all the big hair and but-toned-up collars. Rob was wondering how long his business would last. "The rents are getting higher and higher, and business is not what it was. Besides, everyone is switching over to the compact disc format."

I talked about my hopes for film school. But I wondered if my aunt would go for it. I hadn't told her, but I couldn't dream of doing anything else with my life.

"Just tell her this is what you want to do with your life, Roddy," Erika encouraged.

"It's your life, kid. You have to follow your dreams," Rob stated.

"Did you ever have dreams, Rob?" I asked.

"After Woodstock, I was drafted into the service. I wanted to head for Canada, but I didn't like the idea of running, so I went into the Army. Fortunately for me, I was only there for two years and I never got over to Vietnam. I was stationed over in Germany. After I got out, I was tired of the military bullshit. I decided to go back to being a hippie. I formed a band with some other guys, and we were pretty good. We played psychedelic blues rock, which was big in those days. We were actually signed to Epic Records, but before we could record an album, the band split up. We were all doing too many drugs, no longer taking it seriously. When we recorded the album, the results showed and the record company was so pissed off at us that they never released the album, and they dropped us. And we started fighting, blaming one another for what had happened with the record. It got so bad, we got into fistfights and I had enough. So I became a drifter, wandering the country.

"Then, about '74, I came back to the Lower East Side. I started working in this record shop, while gigging with other guys. A few years later, I raised enough money to buy this record shop from the owner, who retired to Florida. Yeah, I had dreams, but they didn't work out. But that doesn't mean you shouldn't pursue yours."

That was a sobering lesson. I wouldn't tell Rob this, but he made me afraid of getting into drugs. Obviously, drug use did play a role in his band's demise. How could you go from having a major record deal to losing it?

Erika had something going on that night with her girlfriends. I had no plans, but I wanted to hang around in the city. It was a nice night weatherwise, in the 60s, and the NYU college crowd was all about. I found myself wandering over to the West Village, where I happened upon an outdoor cafe on Christopher Street. I sat down, ordered a coffee and apple pie, and decided to people watch.

It wasn't long before a young man about 21 decided to sit down near me. All the outdoor seats and tables were taken up. He asked me politely if he could take the seat, and I said yes.

He asked me if I came to this cafe often, and I said, "No, I just got off work and I was just walking around."

"My name is Cal," the college student announced as he extended his hand toward me for a handshake. I took the hand. It was firm and strong. Cal was from Ohio. He was rather gawky and tall, but clean-cut in the all-American way. He asked where I went to college, and I told him I didn't, that I was in the final semester of my high school year.

"Oh, wow," he exclaimed. "Do you live in the city?"

"No, I live out in Valley Stream, Long Island." I made it up. I really didn't feel like divulging myself to a stranger, as nice as he seemed. Cal was very inquisitive, but it was nice to talk to someone rather than go home back to Staten Island.

"I love New York City," Cal enthused. "I'm from Steubenville, Ohio, and it's so boring there. After I graduate college, I'm going to live here."

"What's your major?" I asked, being the inquisitive one for a change.

"I'm majoring in marketing. What about you? What are you planning to do after high school?"

I gave him my garbage man spiel, on how I loved the aroma of orange juice and grass mingling together on a hot, humid morning.

"Eww, that is so gross, but you are so funny, so cute."

"Cute." That was the word that sent off alarm bells in my mind. This guy was gay and was probably wanting to hook up with me. But it wasn't my thing. I preferred soft, feminine-type bodies compared to masculine, hairy ones. As nice as he was, this was a conversation that wasn't going to last for long. I didn't want to lead this guy on any further.

The bill came. I paid my share of the money and decided to bolt. "Excuse me, but I have to get home. I have to get up tomorrow morning for church."

"Church?" the man tasted the words in confusion. "You're a — you're not gay?"

"Nope, it's not my thing," I said as I stood up from the table.

"But how do you know if you've never tried?" Cal tried to reason with me.

"Maybe I have," I said. It was a line from the movie *Tightrope*, when Clint Eastwood's character is propositioned by a gay man. It was bullshit on my part, but I didn't want any part of this.

"You're a homophobe!" Cal yelled.

I just looked at him as if he were crazy and walked briskly away.

"That's right, walk away!" he yelled further, causing a scene with passersby looking at us.

"Stop being so repressed. You know you're gay. You're just afraid. You can run, but you can't hide." This was all too weird for me. I immediately ran for the next subway station. I got into a conversation with a guy who turned out to be gay, and he was mad at me for not sharing his lifestyle. Maybe he had been rejected too many times, but that wasn't my problem. I caught the 7 train that would take me to Battery Park. I managed to get on the rear car of the train, which held only two other people, a young yuppie couple.

The yuppies got off at the next stop, and I was already well into the intro of the Yes track "Heart of the Sunrise" playing on my on my Walkman. Just a few seconds later, I felt a hard fleshy hand punch me on the left cheek. I bolted up from my bliss and noticed a scraggily haired, bearded, filthy man whose aroma was pungent and clothes were filthy. He lunged for my Walkman, but I wrested it out of his hands; and I started pounding him on the head with it, until it smashed into pieces and was rendered useless as a battering tool.

My mind flashed: "The gun. Use the gun." I had it in my jacket pocket and immediately took it out, proceeding to batter the man's head with it. I had already caused a gash on his forehead with the Walkman, but I busted the gash open even wider with the gun, drawing blood. I turned my attentions to his face, whacking the gun against his nose. The blood trickled down from his nostrils, but I wasn't finished. I concentrated on his head and face. The man was staggering before the thrashing, obviously drunk; but after the thrashing I was giving him, he collapsed to the floor of the train, his face and head a bloody mess.

I was taken aback by what I had done, but I had to gather myself together. I picked up the pieces of the Walkman and stuffed them behind my jacket. I wiped the gun with a handkerchief that I carried in my back pocket and placed it in my inner jacket. I tried wiping my hands off with the handkerchief before the train pulled into the next stop. The handkerchief was slipped into my jacket pocket, and I moved myself into the next cart before the train stopped at Battery Park. There was no hesitation in hightailing it out of the train toward the ferry terminal. The boat coming in from Staten Island was just docking into Manhattan, so I would just about make it. I found myself a seat against the window of the boat, and I was shaking uncontrollably. The waterworks flowed from my eyes. My emotions were rubbed raw.

I'm sure there were passersby looking at me curiously, but I kept my eyes averted toward the window. I didn't want a soul to approach me.

There was the familiar voice of the ferry shoeshine man, calling out "Shine." I even saw a homeless man shuffling along. There had been a time when I wouldn't have hesitated to give change to the homeless, but now I looked upon them with contempt. If the homeless man had simply asked me for the Walkman, I would have considered giving it to him. But instead, he wanted to pound me for it. Was that person who was shuffling along be the next freak to try to hurt me?

After getting off the ferry, I made my bus connection; and when I arrived home, it wasn't a moment too soon. Aunt Jane was sacked out on the couch, the TV blaring. I simply went up to bed and cried myself to sleep. I almost shitted myself the next morning when I saw the *Daily News* and on Page 3 was an article with the headline "Homeless Man Beaten on Subway":

"Commuters at the Battery Park station found a homeless man bleeding heavily from head wounds on the southbound 7 train at about 10:20. The man, George Raif, 43, was taken to St. Vincent's Medical Center, where he was listed in stable condition. Raif was reported to have a blood alcohol level of .03 in his system. He kept repeating to authorities that a kid beat him up. It is believed the suspect departed the train at Battery Park station. Any individual who may have been a witness to the crime can contact the NYPD at 212-345-6556."

Holy shit, I thought to myself. I was merely defending myself, and the police were looking for me. Why weren't they looking out for me when this homeless person punched me in the face?

I hadn't wanted to hurt the man, but he attacked me. I had already been a victim of violent crime twice in that year alone, and as luck would have it, I was struck by lightning again.

My sympathy for the homeless was great. You can design plans for your life, but life never goes according to these plans. For all I knew, I could turn out to be one of the homeless. There are circumstances where drugs and alcohol totally wreck a person's life. Or there could be other factors, such as a bitter divorce or no job.

After that incident, I became wary of the homeless. As mean as it sounds, I wanted no part of them. There were plenty of others who could be sympathetic. I could no longer be one of them.

I didn't bother to tell Aunt Jane. How would she have reacted? Did she need to worry about me more than she did? But I did let loose with the info at the writing workshop that afternoon. It was Brenda's course. Since she wasn't able to get permission from the school to hold a workshop, she decided to hold one unofficially with me and three other students, including Latiesha, the girl in my creative writing class at school. We had gotten along very nicely since we held the same opinions about the Tommasulo stabbing incident. The other two were Lucia, a Hispanic girl in her junior year in high school, and Tommy, a very sophomore who stammered quite a bit. All five of us were in Silver Lake Park that day, sitting on a huge blanket Brenda provided for us, as well as her delicious chocolate chip cookies and iced tea. Brenda lived nearby in one of the apartment houses overlooking the park on Victory Boulevard. As we all sat on the blanket on the slope overlooking the reservoir and with the apartment houses towering above us on the left, I told my tale.

To say that all were mortified would be an understatement. Even Latiesha, who seemed very streetwise, looked at me disbelievingly.

"Oh, my God, Roddy," Brenda exclaimed. "I read about that this morning. You should have called me last night."

I looked down at the blanket, in a very ashamed way. Brenda gently grabbed my chin and brought my eyes to the level of hers.

"You're like family to me, hon. Can't you see that already? Does your aunt know about this?"

"She would have a heart attack if she knew about this. I can't tell her."

Brenda shook her head. "God, this is so surreal what is happening to you. Don't travel alone on the subway at night, please!"

It was akin to having an older sister looking out for her younger brother's every move. I really didn't need the mothering, or to be more succinct, the sistering. I just rolled my eyes upward. Brenda caught this and declared, "Hey, someone has to look out for you, and it might as well be me."

"She's always giving me advice too. It's not just you," Latiesha spoke up.

"You all have incredible potential. The four of you are already good writers. Yes, I started the course for that reason, but there was another reason. You four have so much shit, excuse the language, going on in your lives. If this class provides you with a little bit of pleasure and if it helps cultivate your talents for writing, then I'm thrilled."

Yet Another Adventure

I swear, I was being tested. It was a cool, sunny day in the low 70s. Spring had arrived and I was determined to enjoy it. The unfortunate problem with spring sometimes is that it never lasts long. Summer comes too quickly and it gets unpleasantly hot. I was hoping this wasn't the case that spring, but as long as the weather remained this way, I was determined to enjoy it to the fullest.

I decided to walk along the Midland-South Beach boardwalk, which was run-down looking, and I felt the boards bounce a little as I walked over them.

The cool air was invigorating, and why should I be in a rush to go home? The boardwalk was on the way to my house. South Beach was not too far from Rosebank. My legs were getting a good workout. I had worked on my arms in the weight-training class, but today the legs needed a workout. I planned to take a nap as soon as I got home, before hitting the books.

The beaches had seen better days. Garbage was strewn on the sands, and the water looked brown from a distance. Any person in his or her right mind who lived on Staten Island either went to the Jersey Shore or to Jones Beach out on Long Island for beach swimming. From what I understood, this used to be a popular beach going area back in the '40s, but no more. Neglect and some oil spills from cargo ships have made the beaches less than desirable. I couldn't count out the medical waste scare of 1987 that had an effect on this beach as well as the more desirable beaches along the Jersey Shore. A kid from California who was in my history class exclaimed that the water was all brown. He was right.

I was reaching the end of the boardwalk when I saw a few kids in leather jackets heading my way. They looked to be about my age, but I had such a young face in the day that I looked a few years younger. They were long-haired, wore leather motorcycle jackets with denim vests covering them and torn jeans. They looked like they were a part of the Psychotics, a gang that I had read about in the *Staten Island Advance.*

"Hey look at the faggot," one of the dirtbags mused to his buddies.

My heart went into my mouth and my fists clenched tightly. "Why couldn't I have taken the bus, asshole?" my mind screamed.

"What are you doing, fag?" another asked as the group got closer to me. The third one snickered and smacked his palm against my head.

They all laughed at their brilliance. A bunch of tough assholes only when they were in a gang, but never by themselves. I wished I could punch the living shit out of all three of them, but I knew I'd get beaten badly. But I was going to get a beating whether I wanted to fight or not.

My mind clicked. The gun. I had it in my bag.

"Ooohhh," one of the mental giants smirked, "he's going to hit us with a book."

I whipped out the .9 millimeter. "Let's see you dicks dance," I announced. I aimed at their feet and fired the pistol. The noise was deafening, scaring the shit out of the so-called Psychotic gang members.

"Holy fuckin' shit! He's got a gun. Let's get the fuck out of here!" They ran as fast as they could off that boardwalk and onto Father Capodano Boulevard all the way to Sand Lane. I started to hightail it myself off that boardwalk. There was no one around at that end of the boardwalk except for the gang members and myself. We were at the edge where nobody really ventured. There were people well down the boardwalk, however, who had heard the gunshots and were looking my way. They were quite a distance away, at least four blocks, but I ran all the same. My legs carried me as far as they could to the nearest bus stop on Capodano Boulevard.

The seven minutes I was waiting for the bus seemed an eternity. I was only too glad to get on and all the while I wondered if anyone on that boardwalk had seen me. I was sweating profusely, and the bus driver and about six passengers eyed me suspiciously.

When I reached home sweet home after climbing the steep incline on St. John's Avenue from my drop-off on Bay Street, I was drenched in sweat. I took off my jacket, headed for the kitchen sink and grabbed some good old NYC tap water. After I was able to catch my breath, I collapsed to the couch, too exhausted to be nervous or shaky at that moment. I didn't want to hurt anyone, never mind kill. But those thugs made it so hard on me. I grabbed the gleaming metallic faux pistol from my jacket pocket and wondered if I could ever shoot anyone if I had the bullets. But the faux pistol saved my life! I could have been beaten up pretty badly by the gang, and all anyone could say to me was, "Sorry." I was tired of sympathy. I didn't want any more kicks or punches to the body or head. I was tired of being a victim.

Of course, this was something I had to keep to myself. It was a reasonable facsimile of a handgun and it was still illegal within city limits. Fortunately, I didn't make the news the next day.

Marking the Days

It was already May and the spring weather was heating up. Temperatures were hovering near 80 degrees. At this point, I really wanted to be done with school. I was merely coasting, totally detached from my classes, save for weight training and Brenda's class. I wasn't doing badly, getting marks above 85 in all my classes, except one: typing. Mrs. Welsh couldn't help but notice my inattentiveness, and it irritated her. I was staring out the window on a mild, sunny spring day, wishing I could just be outside.

"You know, young man," Mrs. Welsh spat out, "all you do is sit. I would like to know what is so fascinating outside that window."

The world outside was definitely more fascinating than this class was. "What do you expect me to do, Mrs. Welsh, stand?"

"Don't get me smart with me, Mr. McPherson. Most of the time, you are not doing the assignments, and whatever you happen to do, your work is lousy. You're on notice. If you don't clean up your act, you will fail this class, and then you won't be able to graduate."

That was pure bullshit about the graduation. This class was an elective and not a requirement for graduation. She just didn't want to look bad if I didn't pass her class. Word processors were in vogue at the time, and was it really necessary for me to learn typing on an old Underwood? This class was definitely archaic. I vowed at that very moment that one day I was going to save up enough money to buy a word processor where I wouldn't have to worry about using Wite-Out or toss a page away in frustration whenever a mistake was made. And best of all, I wouldn't have this old biddy on my case: "Mr. McPherson, stop looking at the keyboard." "Mr. McPherson, why are you staring out the window?"

If I failed the class, I wouldn't shed any tears. But I wouldn't look to fail it on purpose. I would try my best. If typing out pages that were mistake-laden satisfied the woman, then so be it.

'Battle of the Bands' Night

"What's wrong, Roddy?" Erika asked.

We were in the record shop taking in *Dark Side of the Moon*. "The Great Gig in the Sky" was playing and after it faded, I turned the stereo off.

"Erika, how do you feel about me?"

"What do you mean?"

"We went out to dinner a couple of weekends ago. Why did we do that?"

Erika was unsure of where this was leading. "Because we're friends, right, Roddy?"

Then she realized what I was trying to ask. "Oh, you thought that."

"Well, I joked about wanting to go to California with you, and you said that you wish you could take me."

"Oh. I broke up with my boyfriend just this past week. We weren't getting along, and I really didn't have a good time out in L.A. It's been like that for some time. I'd much rather have you out there, but not like that. I'm sorry I gave you mixed signals."

"No, my fault," I insisted. "It's just that I see everyone around me is attached, and I feel left out."

"Don't feel so bad; I broke up with my boyfriend that weekend. I don't have anyone myself. You'll find somebody; don't worry. But sometimes you are better off. You can have freedom and see whomever you want without any questions. Mark got too possessive, and I couldn't take it. But you're a really sweet guy. I'm sure you'll hook up with somebody."

Why the hell couldn't it be her? I tried to take heart in Erika's cheering up, but still, it would have been nice to go out on a date and have someone of the opposite sex say "I love you" besides your aunt. On that humid, rainy May night was the storied "battle of the bands" at CBGB's. Killian's band and Erika's were on the lineup. I hadn't seen Killian in a month, and I genuinely enjoyed the guy's company. But unfortunately, he was in a foul mood, and while a witty fellow, his wit was laced with anger on this night.

"Rossi is such a prima donna conceited scumbag," Killian fumed. "We played a gig last week in Queens out on Bell Boulevard, and these two older guys were in the audience. They were musicians. I would say they were in their late 20s. They came up to me after the gig was over and offered me the lead guitar slot in the band they have. Like an asshole, I turned them down, telling them I was committed to my band. I told Rossi all this, and the dick weed tells Frank and Dave that those two guys were considering *him* as the lead singer. He also tells Frank and Dave that those two guys thought I sucked as a guitarist."

"Who told you all this?" I asked.

"Frank and Dave. This was after I told them that I turned those guys down and I would never leave them in the lurch."

"You should have taken that offer. You're much better than that loser band you're in."

Killian was in no mood for "coulda, woulda, shoulda." "Don't remind me, Roddy, all right? I feel lousy enough already. We were in the recording studio today, and Rossi was singing along to "Here I Go Again." I hate that friggin' song as it is, but this moron massacres it. David Coverdale, he's not. He's more like a pimple on Coverdale's ass."

The show had to go on. Rob and I stood by the bar amid the punk hordes. We really stood out in the crowd. The 40-ish hippie and the kid, brown hair cascading just below the collar, wearing a dungaree jacket and Beatles T-shirt. But everyone left us alone. Most knew Rob since they always came to his store, searching for that lost Siouxsie or Buzzcocks album, and most knew me due to my minor celebrity status as Erika's hero. If we weren't recognized, I'm sure this crowd would have smashed bottles all over my head. It was a crowd of mohawks, multicolored spiked hair, dog collars and leather.

The first band up was kids who were younger than me. They called themselves Meat Cleaver and the songs were a barrage of noise. This all culminated when they brought out a horse's head, started chopping it up with cleavers and tossed it into the audience.

Rob stood there smoking his "J," asking aloud, "What the fuck?"

Even I was flabbergasted. "Where the fuck did they find a horse's head?"

"A slaughterhouse," Rob answered.

Erika's band, Catharsis, was up next. Killian decided to watch their set with us, and it was here we got to see Erika and her band in all their death glory, obsessive fashion. She started off with New York Poet Jim Carroll's "People Who Died" song.

"These are people who died, died, died," Erika cried out the chorus.

Rob was taking a few more hits off his joint and muttered "Fucked up!"

Killian just shook his head after that song. "No talent whatsoever, man."

Another memorable song, if you could call it that, was "I wanna kill myself and die."

"I wanna kill myself and die. You can't pass my sadness by. This living is all a lie. I'm not getting a natural high. I wanna kill myself and die, die, die! Die! Die! Die!"

"This chick is whacked," Rob decided.

"Unbelievable," Killian muttered.

Erika came up to us after the set and sought out our opinions. "So, what didja think?"

"That sucked," Rob proclaimed. "You call that talent? What is that crap? 'I wanna kill myself and die'? You need a few tokes of this, sister."

"Oh, fuck you Rob," Erika said. "You wouldn't know good music."

"Good music?" Rob sputtered. "I'm stoned, lady, but I still know the difference between good music and shit like that. You're fucked up!"

"We are all fucked!" Erika screamed. "I just saying it the way it is."

"Is your life that bad?" I asked. "Do you really feel like dying?"

"It's not that bad," Erika stated, "but it could be better."

"Join the club," Killian intoned.

There were a couple of bands afterward that were just horrible and quite indecipherable to these ears. If I didn't have to wade through this mess in order to get to Killian's band, I would have hightailed it out of there. The quality of the music was amateurish. The Sex Pistols, pre-Sid Vicious, and the Clash at least sounded professional. I wished I was back at either the Genesis concert I saw last year or the ELPowell concert, my very first, which I saw two years ago at the Garden. I couldn't forget that concert. Emerson's rich keyboard tapestries and nimble note playing, Greg Lake's steady bass playing and exquisite acoustic ballads topped off by his awesome vocals, and Cozy Powell's rock-hard, heavy-hitting drum style. This shit that was forced upon me on this night was dreck of the worst degree.

And CBGB's club was nothing more than a glorified dump dive bar mistaken for a historical landmark, all because Blondie, Patti Smith, the Talking Heads, Tom Verlaine, Richard Hell, and the Ramones played there. The Talking Heads and Blondie must have been glad they had graduated to arena status. The CBGB's stage was low, and the club was standing room only, like most dive clubs. It reeked of stale beer, more akin to the smell of piss. If, God forbid, there was ever a fire, no one was getting out of this place alive. You would be crushed to death, as if you weren't getting crushed already by just viewing the concert along with the nitwits pushing against you from behind.

Killian's band, High Octane, was the closing act. They held sway that night, even over Erika's theatrics. It was actually the dissolution of his band, and you had to be insensible not to notice the tension between Killian and Rossi. There was Rossi, attempting to sing his heart out, letting out David Lee Roth-style whoops. I saw Killian yell something out to Rossi; and from the anger showing on Killian's face, it no doubt wasn't a compliment. After they had performed the Sex Pistols' "Anarchy in the U.K.," Rossi made an announcement to the crowd.

"Excuse me, everyone, excuse me. Our lead guitar player, Brian Killian, has something to say. He's being a bit of a dickwad, so I just thought I'd ask him to make an idiot out of himself even more."

Killian's retort was quick: "The biggest dick on stage happens to be a prima donna pretending to be a lead singer but fucking it all up as usual. I don't have to make an idiot out of myself on stage.

You're perfectly capable of doing that on your own, and you're succeeding."

Loud cries of "Oooohhh" rang throughout the crowd. Some of the morons in the audience started to yell out, "Fight, fight, fight!" "Smack the shit out of him!" "Kick his fuckin' ass in!"

Rossi was taken aback by Killian's retort. "What the fuck is your problem, man? We're trying to play a gig here!"

"You're my problem," Killian fumed. "You're a backstabbing, cock-sucking moron who is two-faced and full of shit. I heard you've been talking shit about me, and if you want to talk more shit about me, say it to my face."

The crowd wasn't interested in music; they wanted to see a fight onstage. Could I blame them? The music sucked big-time, so they needed another diversion. Chants of "Fight, fight, fight!" started up again. One blithering idiot screamed out, "Kill each other, ya faggots!"

The three of us, Rob, Erika and myself, watched all of this in dismay.

"Holy shit, man," Rob muttered.

"Oh my God," Erika exclaimed. "Is this for real?"

I shook my head sideways. It was all coming to a head. There had been resentment building between Killian and Rossi for some time. I just didn't think it would happen onstage at an important gig. At one point between songs, Killian and Rossi walked over to each other and started to exchange words. The bouncers had to jump onstage and intervene. They also suggested that if Killian and Rossi wanted to engage in fisticuffs, they were better off doing it outside of the club.

"This isn't over," Rossi proclaimed.

"Damn straight," Killian shot back, the only agreement they had all night.

The band played on, but dispirited, lacking in energy and definitely wishing they were elsewhere. In fairness, Killian's band was not my cup of tea, but there were gigs where I was impressed by the high energy and the professionalism of Killian and Frank Calico, the bass guitarist. Despite the singer's and drummer's shortcomings, it sounded at least halfway professional; and with a lineup of bands such as this, they should have won the competition easily. The enthusiasm and energy were definitely lacking within the band. They closed out their set with their signature song, "Freaks and Geeks," a satire about Staten Island metalheads and guidos.

Boos rang out throughout the crowd. There were still chants calling for a fight between Killian and Rossi. The band had tanked. The looks of disgust on the bandmates' faces was apparent. What happened next took me by surprise, and I had been privy to Killian's discussion about his band. He took his guitar and whacked Rossi over the head, eliciting a loud roar of approval from the crowd. Rossi tumbled to the stage floor, knocked out cold. Then Killian simply walked off stage.

Rossi had to be helped by a couple of bouncers. I t appeared his head was bleeding. All the bands were brought back onstage, except for Rossi, recuperating in the backstage area. The contest was to be decided by audience applause. Would you believe Killian's band got the most applause, all because of the guitarist swinging at the lead singer's head as if he were Mike Schmidt connecting with a fastball?

The whole place erupted into a frenzied cheer. There was much hollering and whooping. By whooping, I'm talking about that infamous cheer the audiences used on the then-popular *Morton Downey Jr. Show*: "Wooo! Woo! Woo! Woo!"

Rob appeared to be one of the more sensible people in this dive club. "No wonder I don't listen to today's music," he said, shaking his head in disbelief. Even the joints he was smoking were not dulling the pain of this concert for him.

Erika, for her part, was dismayed that Killian's band could win such an award for the guitarist slamming his musical instrument over the lead singer's head.

"Fuck!" she screamed. "This is such bullshit."

The fight between Rossi and Killian had only begun. We were outside, and Rossi wasn't going to let that guitar shot go. Rob, Erika and I went through the alleyway where the bands loaded up their gear into their vehicles, and we saw Rossi on top of Killian, trying to smash his head against the ground. A small crowd, namely the other bands, had gathered around the two combatants.

I would have thought Rossi would pound the shit out of Killian. He had at least a thirty-pound advantage over the guitarist. But with surprising agility he pushed off Rossi and gave him a well-placed kick to his solar plexus. After that maneuver knocked the wind out of Rossi, Killian followed up with a haymaker to Rossi's face, knocking him out for the second time that evening. To add insult to injury, Killian spat on him.

"I quit," yelled Killian to the fallen singer, and to Frank and Dave, who were looking at all of this action in wide-eyed horror. "You guys get yourself another guitarist. I'm not massaging anyone else's ego. Fuck that!"

I approached Killian. "Brian, let's get out of here. Why don't we get something to eat? Hang out with us."

"Fuck it all," Killian said in disgust. "Let me get my guitar."

The four of us, Erika, Killian, Rob and myself, had dinner at a greasy spoon. The conversation started out with good-natured ribbing from Erika toward Killian.

"I actually hated that you guys won. I mean, a fistfight? You've gotta be kiddin' me. But than I saw you guys fighting outside, and I felt bad."

"Erika, you can have my share of the prize money," Killian said. "I should have gotten out months ago."

"Hey, maybe you can hook up with those two guys still?" I offered.

Killian was pessimistic about that. "They probably chose someone already for the slot. I worked so hard with that band, and it was just a waste, wasn't it?"

"It couldn't have been a waste," Rob pointed out. "You had more good times than bad, right? You got good stage experience as a musician, right?"

Killian nodded. "It was good for all of that."

We all talked over the food about our ambitions for the future. Rob talked about retiring, moving up to Vermont in five years. And despite being a stoner, he was pretty lucid in what he was saying. "New York is going down the tubes. Rents are skyrocketing, the crime is out of control. Who needs this? I'm going to run a bed and breakfast up in Vermont. In five years, I'm getting out."

Erika talked about the fashion industry. "I'm not serious about music, but I want to design. There's too many poets already. I'm not a singer, and to tell you the truth, I think I'm over my obsession with death. The negativity got to me tonight. I want to live to a ripe old age, but I'll do it my way. Clothes are always going to be in demand, so I won't have to worry about starving."

Killian stated music is his life. "I'll finish up school and take it from there. Perhaps I'll move out to Seattle. The music scene is starting to grow out there. The heavy metal scene out in L.A. is going to die out."

I listened to all what was being said. I was not going to volunteer any info, but Erika asked me.

"It would be great if I could go to film school, if my aunt lets me."

"Tell her it's what you want to do more than anything else in the world," Erika suggested.

It would be a tough sell, but I had to convince my aunt that there was nothing else I wanted to do but break into the film world. I loved movies, I loved writing screenplays, and it was a natural fit.

"I want to see what you wrote," Erika clamored. "What are you afraid of?"

"He's afraid of being laughed at," Killian chimed in. "I read one of his screenplays. It's a *Death Wish*-type movie, and it was pretty good."

It was a weird but wonderful night. One of those nights with friends you wish you could always have.

And it extended into Sunday afternoon with another group of people I was fond of: Brenda, Latiesha, Lucia and Tim. Tim was quieter than me, partly because he stuttered and stammered. I felt for him, because I had that same problem in junior high into my freshman year of high school, but I had taken the time to keep whatever speech I had to say economical and to the point. It was usually one-word answers, and that made me appear to be some sort of weirdo, but I didn't want to look like an idiot, even though stuttering and stammering is nothing to be ashamed of. It happens to people. Tim wrote a wonderful essay about feeling self-conscious about his stuttering and how he felt so inept. Kids often teased him about it, and I felt really bad about it. We all did. I wished I could protect him against those bastards abusing him.

Brenda counseled him as best as she could. "Just because you have a speech impediment doesn't mean you can't overcome it. You can, and you will."

Lucia wrote about her father abusing her mom. It was such a sad and sick tale. At one point, Lucia broke down while reading this, and Brenda told her that if she didn't wish to continue further, she did not have to. Lucia, trooper that she was, finished. Brenda gave her a supportive hug.

Latiesha talked about her crack addict brother and how her mom had kicked him out of their apartment. He had broken into the apartment a couple of times, stealing money and threatening Latiesha, her younger sister and her mom with a knife. That was a harrowing tale, just as harrowing as Lucia's tale of her father.

I wrote about how I had two great support groups in the friends I had in Rob, Erika and Killian and in this writing group where a teacher encouraged our budding talents. I was saddened by the horror stories of Lucia and Latiesha, and could I help them — and how?

I was a bit depressed about those tales, and I felt very lucky to be me. On the next day, I asked Brenda if there was anything she could do for Latiesha and Lucia.

"I can't really do a whole lot, Roddy," she said sadly. "With Lucia, I'm not at liberty to discuss it, but I have tried going through the proper channels. And as far as Latiesha is concerned, there's not much there I can help with. A lot of this is out of my hands."

Brenda went on. "I'm just a teacher. I'm not a social worker or a police officer. But it doesn't mean I care any less about them. After that horrible fight last year between those two boys, I vowed never to care."

"That's why you're such a good teacher," I remarked. I wished I could tell her I loved her for caring, but I felt embarrassed about displaying affection.

A Sitdown Talk with Aunt Jane

I was eating dinner in the kitchen later that night, and Aunt Jane asked me about my plans after graduation. "It's getting close to that time," she said. "What are you planning to do with yourself?"

"I want to go to film school," I said outright.

"Film school?" She tasted the idea unhappily. "You're off your noggin'. You'd best get yourself an education. The arts is no way to make a living. You'll starve to death. Go to a proper school, why don't ye."

I was getting pissed off. It was my life, my dream. "Aunt Jane, you were young once. Didn't you have a dream?"

"Ye know I used to act onstage long before ye were born. I was always on Broadway in drama plays, but I wanted to settle down and have a normal life. Rather than keep going on with it, I gave it up. It became rather grueling. I got married to a bus driver, became a housewife and a mom."

"Aunt Jane, you never had any kids."

"I did Roddy, well before ye came to live with us. Your cousin Catherine. She was only 6 years old when she died. She was sick for a while, the poor thing. She had heart failure."

"How many years ago was this?"

"We are talking about July 16, 1973. Almost 15 years ago."

"You never told me this."

"I didn't want to go on reminding meself of all this. It is so damned depressing to think about how you outlived your own flesh and blood that you gave birth to. What good would it be for ye to know about it? What good would it do for ye? Ye didn't have an easy childhood growing up."

It wouldn't have done me any good. The one thing I missed about the Bronx was Jasmine Flores. I was pretty much a lonely kid growing up on Staten Island. I was only friends with Killian because my aunt was friends with his mom.

"Do you think about her?" I asked about the child.

"Once in while, and it still hurts. It was much worse after she died. I was in grief for months. Ye never get over it, but I try not to think about it so much. I think about it a lot on your cousin's birthday, April 30, and her date of death, July 16."

"I'm sorry, Aunt Jane. I never knew."

"It's not your fault. But the reason why I get on ye sometimes is because ye became a son to me. I made a promise to your mother I would take care of ye. I don't think I've done a bad job, have I?"

No, she hadn't. There were times in those years I definitely didn't appreciate my aunt. I thought of her as a nag, uncool and a pain in the rear. But I would miss her terribly if anything happened to her.

"Aunt Jane, thanks for looking after me all these years."

"I wanted to." She gave me a hug, which she rarely did. I wasn't much for physical contact either, and I probably got that trait from her.

I guess we were all good in that family at suppressing our emotions, and the more I thought about it, I was impressed with Aunt Jane's stoic demeanor. She didn't ever want to be seen as falling apart. And except for when my Uncle Harry died, she was never a crier.

"If film school is what you really want to do for yourself, then do it. I don't know if I can afford it, but I'll see what I can do. I'd rather see ye happy. But there will be lots of frustrations in that life. Just make sure you never give up on yerself and work hard. Always work hard."

My aunt showed me a photo album of her that depicted her stage days. She was into dramatic acting, but you never would have thought such a seemingly no-nonsense person had been into the theater. By the time I came to live with her, her acting days were 10 years behind her.

"The life is a struggle, and you'll never make a lot of money in the arts. Think about doing something else."

There was nothing else I could think of.

That Sinking Feeling

It was 10:30 on a Thursday evening when I received a phone call. I was in bed, reading a movie tie-in book of *Fort Apache: The Bronx*, when my aunt called up to me. "Roddy, it's yer boss at that record shop; don't stay up too late."

I wondered what Rob wanted. He had never called me at home.

"Hey, Roddy."

"Hey Rob, what's going on?"

"Did you hear?" Rob's voice was solemn.

"Hear what?"

"Erika. She was killed just a couple of hours ago. Some maniac pushed her onto the tracks in front of a subway train."

My heart went into my mouth. "No, no way, man, no. This is a joke, right, Rob?"

"I wouldn't kid around like that, Roddy. You know that. And I'm as sober as a judge right now. It's been on the 10 o'clock news, Channel 5. You'll probably catch it again at 11, and I'm sure the story will be in the papers tomorrow."

"Who did this?" I demanded in anguish.

"Some psychopath. Maybe hopped up on crack, or some mental patient. They don't know too many details about the guy who did this. But whatever, he's a whack job, man."

I was too upset to speak any further about the matter. There was a long pause in the conversation.

"Roddy, I'm sorry," Rob intoned, his voice breaking.

"I'm sorry too," I said numbly.

"Listen, if you don't want to come in Saturday, I understand. I can handle it by myself."

What was I going to do, just sit around my house and mope? "It's all right. I'd rather come in."

"All right, but if you change your mind, let me know."

"Don't worry about it. I'll be there.

"Okay, man, I'll see you on Saturday. We'll talk more about this."

I watched the 11 o'clock news to see for myself. I didn't want to believe it. But it was true:

"A Brooklyn woman was pushed off a subway platform on 23rd Street in Manhattan tonight. At 8:47 p.m., 19-year-old Erika Nielsen was waiting at the East 23rd Street subway platform when a homeless man, 43-year-old Wesley Wescott, shoved her onto the tracks in front of an oncoming train, bound for Brooklyn. The victim died instantly.

"The suspect has had a long history of psychiatric troubles. He is being held in police custody at Bellevue Hospital for further psychiatric evaluation."

"God in heaven, help us," Aunt Jane said. "I'm so sorry, Roddy."

There was a steel ball sitting in the pit of my stomach. A wave of nausea came over me, and I made a beeline for the upstairs bathroom. A river of vomit came flowing out of me. I leaned over the toilet bowl doing my best to grip it, but I collapsed to the tile floor.

The next day was senior day, an unofficial holiday for the senior classmen. I took the day off not because I was honoring that tradition but out of respect for Erika. I told my aunt what I was doing and how it wouldn't have made sense for me to go to school. There would be no kind of serious learning going down.

My aunt was having none of it. "What are ye going to do, sit around here and mope? Senior day? What kind of garbage is that? It's a regular school day, and yer going to school."

Fine. But instead of boarding the bus for Normand High, I boarded the bus for Bay Ridge, Brooklyn, home of Erika. I just wanted to walk in her neighborhood, and somehow obtain a connection with her, if that was possible. That connection exists only in the movies, where you can hold conversations with the dead. I walked around Bay Ridge. Erika had lived in one of those apartment complexes overlooking the Narrows with a spectacular view of the harbor. I walked along the Shore Park walkway underneath the Verrazano Bridge that stretched to the top edge of Bay Ridge, just losing myself in my thoughts. The day was breezy, sunny and warm.

I sat down on a bench that overlooked the harbor, and that numbness I had was lingering along with the steel ball in my stomach. I'm just not a crier, especially when it comes to mourning. I had reacted the same way the previous year, when Uncle Harry passed on. Everyone is different when it comes to mourning. Erika was really down to earth, and it didn't matter what background you had, she could hold a conversation with anyone. Her murder was so senseless, which made this all the harder to accept, but murders never make sense, do they?

I purchased a hot dog from a nearby stand, forcing myself to eat something, but I had a hard time swallowing that down — like I had with this recent tragedy. Not long after that, I returned home. The day was golden sunshine, but it might as well have been murky, cloudy skies for all I cared.

On the bus ride back to Staten Island, I thought about the people I had lost in my life: my father, my mother, my uncle and now Erika. I wondered if I was cursed, where people around me just have a habit of dying.

The story was all over the news, and I'm sure Brenda must have known about it. Since I wasn't in class that day, Brenda would put two and two together, and figure out why I wasn't there. She knew I wouldn't be taking off because of senior day. And I knew she would try to call my house to see how I was doing. She did call around 5. My aunt was home and answered.

"Hello, young lady, how are ye? It's so good to hear from ye. When are ye going to have dinner with us again? I'd really like to have ye over soon."

There was a pause. "You drive yerself so hard, young lassie, but your hard work will pay off. I tell Roddy he should copy ye more often."

There was another pause and more laughs. "Oh, okay, I'll get Roddy. You take care of yourself, dear. Bye."

Aunt Jane handed the phone off to me. "It's yer teacher, Brenda. She's a sweetheart."

I took the phone. "Hello."

"Hey, Roddy. I guess you know what I'm calling about. How are you holding up?"

"Horrible, just horrible," I said as I took the cordless phone upstairs to my room.

"I wouldn't have bothered calling you since it's senior day today, but I was concerned about you. Roddy, I'm so sorry, hon." Her voice started to break. "I really liked that girl. This is so friggin' senseless! I had to keep myself from crying today."

"I should have been there, Brenda. I should have been there. What kind of a sick bastard does a thing like that? They should hang that mother fucker by his cock."

"Roddy, how could you have known that some psycho fuck would push Erika off a subway platform." Brenda's sadness was turning into anger. "You're not clairvoyant. If we all were, we would be able to save the lives of people we love. It doesn't work that way."

"I talked to her last week. She didn't want to die. She talked about fashion designing and how she couldn't wait to set her mark on the fashion world."

"It's funny," Brenda spoke. "She called me just the day before, asking me if I still held writing classes. It was a nice conversation, and she read me a poem about waltzing in a flower bed. It was so positive and so spiritual. Then I find out two days later she's dead. I'm just as upset as you are."

"I'm not coming, Sunday, Brenda. I'm just not up to it," I announced.

"Roddy, that's entirely up to you, hon. But just know this: you are among friends, and we're there for you if you need us. If you need me, you know where to reach me. Take care of yourself, and I'll see you in class Monday."

"And Brenda... Thanks for covering for me."

"Don't mention it. Anytime."

I called Rob later that night and told him I would be late coming in the next day. I had plans.

"You don't have to come in if you don't want to, Roddy."

"I'll be there, about 12 or 1 o'clock, Rob. I have to take care of something."

Return to Highbridge

That "something" I was talking about with Rob involved me going to the Bronx in my old neighborhood of Highbridge. The reason: Erika's death got me to thinking about some of the people in my life and how they just weren't there anymore, namely my father, my mom, my uncle and now Erika. Brenda was a friend, but what was going to happen to that friendship when school was over? Killian looked to be more available since his band fell apart, but how long would that last? He was a good musician, so it wouldn't be long before he found another band, and I would hardly see him anymore.

I needed a life, but high school didn't provide that for me. My whole life was the record shop and Brenda's Sunday writing class. Maybe things would be different once I graduated high school.

But why wait? I remembered Jasmine and how much she took care of me back in the day. I wondered if she was still alive and if she was still in the Bronx. I had to find out. Maybe I could rekindle that friendship again. We never had kept in touch after her family dropped me off on my first day of living with my aunt and uncle on Staten Island.

It wasn't the safest of trips. The neighborhood had gotten worse since I left. Crack cocaine had reared its ugly head in the South Bronx as it had in many ghetto areas in NYC. Riding the subway into those areas was not the most sensible idea I ever had, but how the hell was I going to get up there? My aunt would have been suspicious as to why I was using the car.

I felt very comforted by the faux .9 millimeter I had hidden in my jacket. It was a cloudy day, very overcast and humid. I did feel warm with the black windbreaker I had on, but I needed to conceal that weapon. If any thug even approached me, I was going to shoot first and ask questions later. What was fortunate was that I was traveling early in the morning, when probably most of the riff-raff were still sleeping off last night's excesses. And there were a fair amount of people traveling up there, except I was probably the only white person on the train.

The subway ride was long, at least an hour, to the 170th Street station. In my pockets I had a Bronx street atlas, but I tried to keep it hidden, for fear of looking like a tourist, an easy mark for any thug.

I reached the 170th Street station, which was especially more rundown-looking than the subway stations I had seen in Manhattan. The walls were completely covered in graffiti, and a warning on the wall scrawled in red captured my attention: "Enter at your own risk."

Keeping that in kind, I ascended the steps up to the Highbridge streets.

The Bronx street scene brought back memories as I made my way toward the old homestead on Woodycrest Avenue. Not too many people seemed to be outside on these mean streets this Saturday morning. Old apartment houses stood their ground defiantly amid the poverty, while others were vacant. Either they were burned-out hulks, most likely a breeding ground for addicts, or they were boarded up.

The neighborhood still had its magnificent points: the hilly curved streets and the infamous Highbridge pedestrian walkway bridge. I could see Yankee Stadium not too far away. Perhaps after locating Jasmine, I would attend a game. The Yankees were trying to revitalize themselves under the fourth reign of Billy Martin; and so far, with a team that didn't possess a lot of talent, save for Dave Righetti and Don Mattingly, they were in first place. Even though the pennants had dried up seven years prior, they were still competitive.

My optimism that day was running high with the prospect of meeting up with Jasmine and also attending a ball game at the stadium. I approached 265 Woodycrest, an old tan five-story walkup. I walked up the steps and inside the lobby. Paint was peeling off the walls, and there were cracks as well. The doorbells were all busted, except for the superintendent's. The name plate read "Sanchez." I rang the bell.

"*Uno momento*," rang out a voice through the cackling speaker.

Within a minute, the superintendant came. He was a short, squat, middle-aged and gray-mustachioed man dressed in a plaid flannel shirt and blue work pants.

"Hi. Can you tell me if Jasmine Flores still works here?" I asked.

He gave a look of incomprehension. "Jasmine Flores?"

"The Flores family," I continued. "Do they still live here?"

"No, I no hear of Flores family. Not here."

"I used to live here 11 years ago. They lived here back then."

"*Senor,* I no live here 11 years ago."

"All right, thanks anyway."

I walked outside defeated. They had moved away, and good for them. Why stay in a neighborhood that was deteriorating? If you landed into some money, you'd be a fool to stay in this neighborhood, but I wondered where they could have moved off to.

I wasted a Saturday morning coming up here. Well, not completely. There was Yankee Stadium.

A heavyset woman, pleasant looking, was peering out of her first-story apartment window.

"Excuse me, are you looking for the Flores family?"

"Yeah, how do you know?"

I was just outside my apartment when I heard you and the super talking. That family moved 10 years ago. I think they live in Brooklyn now, but I'm not sure where."

Okay, Brooklyn. But that could be any neighborhood. Perhaps Bushwick or Sunset Park, trading one slum area for another. Who knew? But I could try looking in the Brooklyn phone books.

"Did you use to live here?" the woman asked.

"Eleven years ago. I used to live here with my mom. We were the McPhersons."

It dawned on the woman who I was. "You're Roddy. I remember you and your mom. Your mom was so nice to me. I went into labor in my apartment, and she helped me through it. She was such a nice lady. I'm so sorry she passed away."

"Thanks."

"I bet you don't remember me. My name is Liz Cartegna. I moved up here just a few months before your mom died. I remember that you used to stay with the Floreses, but after your mom died you moved away. Where do you live now?"

"Staten Island."

"You've come a long way, Roddy. But you really should be careful walking around here alone. There are a lot of good people up here, but we also have problem people: crack addicts, youth gangs. Did you take the subway up here?"

"Yeah."

"Papi, that is so dangerous. You could get really hurt."

"I'm okay. I used to live up here."

"But this neighborhood is a lot more dangerous now than it was when you were living here. This crack cocaine garbage is tearing this neighborhood apart."

I shrugged my shoulders. What Liz didn't know was that I had a faux gun in my jacket pocket.

"Why don't you come inside, have a little something to eat," Liz offered.

"No, I better get going. I'm going to go to Yankee Stadium, take in a day game."

"Papi, don't walk around here. It's not safe. Look, come inside, I'm not going to bite."

Liz was a very gracious host, serving up fried plantains for her son and me. Her son, Ivan, was 11. He seemed like a good kid. He was a thin, wiry youth with a pleasant smile. I complimented him on his Don Mattingly T-shirt, and we started talking baseball. I reiterated my plans to go to Yankee Stadium, but Ivan informed me that the team was out of town, playing in Baltimore.

"That's the end of that. I might as well go to work."

"Where do you work?" Liz asked.

"I work in Manhattan at a record store. I did tell my boss I would be delayed today, that I had something to do."

"Do you like it there?" Liz asked.

"I love it there, but my co-worker was killed. She was the girl that was pushed onto the tracks a couple of days ago..."

"Oh my God. I saw that," Liz interrupted. "That was *loco*, really *loco*. Were you two close?"

"We were friends, but not boyfriend/girlfriend. It's going to be hard working without her."

"I'm sorry, honey."

"I wish Jasmine still lived here."

Liz had an idea. "Why don't I search around for Jasmine? You give me your phone number, and I'll let you know if I ever came across her."

I was desperate for any help. And Liz was really a nice lady. She was very heavyset, but she had a pretty, kind face. Liz was dressed in sweats and was barefoot. He apartment was small but very homey. There was a lot of clutter containing magazines and newspapers, and there were Ivan toys, but it wasn't dirty. The kitchen we ate in was white and spotless.

"What grade are you in, Roddy?" Liz asked.

"I'm in my senior year of high school."

"Oh, good for you. Are you planning to go to college?"

Of course, I really want to go to film school, but my aunt may not be able to afford it. "I'll probably just work. I have no talents in anything."

"Oh, that hurts me to hear you say that. You seem well spoken. Isn't there anything you like to do?"

"Well, I write. I'm not very good at it, but my English teacher says I'm good."

"She's probably right. I'm a teacher myself. I teach English as a second language over at the Highbridge Community Center. Then she added proudly, "We teachers are usually right about these things."

"She's the best teacher I've ever had," I stated. "She believes in me. Have you ever heard of Brenda Moriarty?"

I should have known better than to ask that. Just because you're in the education field doesn't mean you necessarily know everyone. But it's a small world:

"Oh, my God, I do!" Liz exclaimed. "We took a writing course together at the Gotham workshop in Manhattan. She is really such a nice person. But I haven't heard from her since then. I understand she had trouble in a school she taught in Brooklyn last year."

"Yeah, she told me about that."

"That was bad for her, but I'm glad she's teaching again. I should give her a call, see how she's doing."

I was curious to hear what other people said about her. "How is Brenda as a writer?" I asked.

"She's really good," Liz enthused. She didn't need the course, but it was something for her to do. She could write a novel if she wanted."

Liz turned her attentions to me. "You should really consider college. You're too smart to waste yourself in a menial labor job."

"I'll try," I said, thinking again of film school.

It was time to leave and go to work. Even if the Yanks had been playing in the Bronx that day, I had already given Rob my word I would be coming in.

"Why don't you give me your phone number?" Liz asked. "I'll try to see if I can contact Jasmine, but I can't make you any promises."

"Okay." Any help was good at this point.

"Will you be okay going to the train station? Do you need a ride?"

"I'll be all right."

"I don't know, Papi; you're *loco* walking around here. You are such an easy mark."

"I can take care of myself," I insisted. "I'm fine."

Liz was unsure. "If you insist. Take care, Roddy. Watch yourself. And you can call me whenever you need to. It was nice meeting you again."

I left the apartment and walked into the Highbridge streets. She wasn't Jasmine, but Liz was really cool, and if she could help me find Jasmine, great. And now this was one more friend than I had before.

Three tough-looking kids, about my age, stood at the corner opposite the subway entrance. They were dressed in baggy hip-hop T-shirts and pants. They were definitely better dressed than the youth gangs I remembered seeing 11 years prior. But they still had the hard looks of those gangs. Their looks gave away the frustration of living in low-income areas such as the South Bronx, and outsiders were not welcome. They walked toward me.

I tensed up. I should have had Liz give me a ride to Manhattan, but I didn't want to put her out. She was a very hospitable lady, but she had done too much for me already.

"What the fuck do ya think you're doin', white boy?" one said in that hard Bronx, Newyorican accent.

"Visiting a friend," I said.

"You don't have fuckin' friends up here, white boy. Your ass don't belong here."

"I used to live here," I said evenly. The three were blocking my way toward the subway entrance.

"You wanna trespass here, you gotta pay us, you fuckin' *puta*," another said.

I took out the small, cold hard steel that had been nestled in my jacket pocket. "Back off, mother fuckers, just back the fuck off or I'll blow you all the fuck away. I'm a pretty good shot and I don't miss." I tried to put on a look of mock fury, but truth be told, I was shitting bricks.

One of them started to chuckle. "You fuckin' stupid, *blanco*, trying to scare us with a water pistol. You gonna die."

Before the fools could make a move on me, I held the gun in the air and pulled back the trigger.

The noise was deafening as it was that day when the Psychotics confronted me. These thugs got the message.

"Holy fuckin' shit! Mother fucker ain't playin' around," one shouted as they ran away from me. I chuckled watching these so-called tough-guy "gangbangers" run away like mice in a field, back among the buildings of the badlands.

I descended the subway steps into the dank, dark, smelly and rancid subway station.

After placing the gun back into my jacket pocket, I caressed it through the jacket.

It was another close call, and as I rode the subway into Manhattan, I thought, "Thank God this gun only fires blanks. If there was the capability of bullets, the results would not have been pretty."

I got to the record shop just before 1 in the afternoon. It had started to rain by the time I walked in. Rob was manning the counter, helping a couple of college students with their purchases of vinyl.

Rob noticed me and nodded. After the students left the store, he told me I hadn't needed to bother to come in. "What am I going to be doing? Sitting at home?" I asked rhetorically.

Maybe I should have. It was strange at times when I found myself looking about for Erika. I expected to see her there right next to me, and a few times I thought I heard her voice. When I had to stop and remind myself Erika was no longer there, I just felt a lot sadder and became depressed.

Six o'clock came around and I wasn't in a mood to stay at the store anymore. Those were the longest five hours I had ever spent. Rob wasn't saying much except to mention that the wake for Erika would be held on Monday and the funeral would be on Tuesday.

I couldn't make the funeral since it was a school day, but I definitely had to attend the wake. I didn't look forward to it. Who does with these things?

I asked Rob if I could go home. "I just can't stay here anymore today," I stated.

"It's rough, man, it's rough," Rob agreed. "I don't think it's ever going to be the same again without her. Thanks for coming in, Roddy. I know it wasn't easy. I don't want to be here, either."

Wild Night Out

My aunt was surprised to see me home early on a Saturday. In her house, she laid down the law with curfews during the week: No going out on a school night, but Fridays and Saturdays were no problem as long as I called to say I was all right; otherwise she would worry. I wasn't always good about calling, and there were times she would give me hell about it. On this night it seemed she didn't have to worry about that — until Killian called while I was eating my steak.

"Hey, what are you going to do, mourn your life away? Let's hang out for a while," Killian suggested.

"No, Brian, I don't feel like it. I'm not feeling well."

"C'mon, it will do you some good to get the hell out of the house."

"I was out of the house, Kevin. I worked today."

"I know that. I called the record shop, and Rob said you left early. But let's hang out awhile. There's a good band I want to check out at The Caves."

"All right," I relented. "Just a couple of hours."

Killian picked me up in his cherry red, restored '73 Ford Mustang. The car was a behemoth. The kid was talented. As well as being an adept musician, Killian was quite handy as a mechanic.

The Caves was a club on Van Duzer Street in the Stapleton section of Staten Island. It was an old historic building, originally a brewery. There were caves actually built into the structure, where beer would be stored away. Then it was a restaurant for a while, a German Hofbräu called Demyans. I had dinner a few times over there with my aunt and uncle. The most significant event was my communion dinner. The place went under after a fire broke out seven years ago, and went through numerous ownerships since then as a club. The neighborhood wasn't the best: A dangerous housing project, the Stapleton houses, was just a few blocks away.

I asked Killian if he was worried about his car as we parked in the massive lot.

"That's why I have this baby," he said, brandishing a red bar with black protruding handles that allowed itself to slip over the steering wheel.

We strolled into the club and watched a pretty good set by the Brooklyn Horns, a band that played jazz, blues and funk. It was a mixture of white guys and black guys playing together, and they jelled real well. My favorite highlight was watching them perform old Chicago warhorses such as "25 or 6 to 4" and "Poem 58." The guitarist had nailed down Terry Kath's parts. I was blown away, and so was Killian, who kept muttering, "Holy shit, these guys are good."

During intermission the booze was making me feel no pain. I jokingly asked Killian about his band.

"You dick," Killian spat out. "The band broke up a week ago. Are you trying to break my balls?"

"Shit, yeah," I said, smiling devilishly. Now the alcohol was making me playful.

"You asshole," Killian remarked. "That shithead Rossi had it coming."

"What about the other band? Did you contact them?"

"Yeah, they filled the spot. Just my fuckin' luck."

We noticed a couple of women in their mid-20s sitting at a table nearby. They were very pretty and absolutely big-haired. That big hair reached mountain-high proportions, but it didn't seem normal. Perhaps my perception of their hair was distorted by my alcohol consumption. Killian had consumed two by this time. I had already consumed four and was working on my fifth. The beer was giving me confidence, which I greatly lacked when I was sober. It also made me open up more to Killian, which was a mistake.

"I went up to the South Bronx today. Remember that girl Jasmine I was telling you about? I wanted to make contact with her."

Killian was incredulous. "You went up there? Are you out of your mind?"

"I knew you wouldn't get it," I said dismissively.

"Get what?" Killian demanded. "Did you go up there by yourself?"

"Yes."

"You're out of your fuckin' mind, man. All for a chick that baby-sat you many moons ago. You're lucky you didn't get the shit kicked out of you all over again. Did you see her?"

"No," I exhaled uneasily.

"Then you wasted your time up there."

"Yes and no."

"What the hell do you mean, 'Yes and no'?"

"No, because I didn't get to see Jasmine. Yes, because when I went up to the apartment building, this lady who lives there remembered me, and she remembered Jasmine. She offered to help me find where Jasmine has gone off to."

"Does she have any idea where?"

"Brooklyn, perhaps."

Now part of me wondered if Jasmine would even care to see me. That was 11 years ago, and you move on with your life. I thought I had, but I wanted to reconnect with what I had. Yes, it was what you would call safe living back in the day, but we were friends, and it was sad we had grown out of touch with one another.

Killian couldn't comprehend it. "Why is it so important for you to meet up with this chick? She has her own life now. What makes you think she has time for you? Do you have a thing for this chick?"

Perhaps broaching this subject was a mistake with this clown. "No, asshole! I lost my father, who I never knew; my mom, who I barely knew; my uncle, who helped raise me; and Erika, who was my best friend other than you. I'm sick and tried of losing people, man. I lost Jasmine, too, but she's probably still alive, and wouldn't it be nice to gain someone back? Maybe I'm jinxed, because every-one I know either dies or disappears."

"Give me a fuckin' break, Roddy. I'm still alive. Your aunt is still alive. Rob is still alive. Stop being so melodramatic."

"Look," I said in exasperation. "Haven't you ever lost anybody? Can you even relate to what the hell I'm saying?"

"I lost my band, Roddy. I know there were problems, but I'm missing those guys, except for Rossi. Who am I kidding, Rossi is a dick, but we did have good times. I'm depressed over that. Now I wonder if I'll get another gig."

"You will," I said affirmatively. You're talented enough."

"Thanks."

During that intermission, a wave of angst fell over me. Even though meeting Liz was cool, I wanted Jasmine and I did fail in that mission. Who the hell knew if Liz could find her. I watched the people at nearby tables chattering away happily. Some were boyfriend/girlfriend, and why couldn't I have that?

"Why the fuck can't I have a girlfriend, Kevin? What the fuck is with me? Do I have to put gallons of Vitalis hair spray in my hair; do I have to drive a car with fuckin' tinted windows?"

My voice was rising and people were starting to look my way. I just didn't care. I was drunk, and in such a horrific mood, I just didn't care about people's perceptions of me at that point. Killian did care, and simply told me to calm down.

"Fuck, no, I won't calm down!" I threw my beer glass to the floor, causing it to shatter, and the place hushed up with all eyes looking at me.

I questioned the gawking onlookers. "What are you looking at, huh? Haven't you seen a drunken Irish man before?"

Killian tried to grab me. "C'mon ,man, let's get out of here!" But I was resisting.

"I'm not fuckin' finished," I snarled. I decided to give the audience a bit of a tirade. "Keep on looking, that's all you're good for, gawking like shitheads. You're too much of lame, dumb fucks to do anything else!"

A bouncer came over to the commotion. He was a huge burly black guy with a no nonsense attitude. "Hey let's go, get that shit out of here, let's go."

Killian interjected. "Leave him alone. I'll get him out of here. His girlfriend passed away. He's really upset."

"Get him out of here, now, or I'll throw his ass out of here," the bouncer demanded.

"Take it easy," Killian said, "we're going. C'mon Roddy, let's go."

Once in the car, Killian tried to get to the bottom of my mood. "What is with you tonight?"

"I told you I didn't want to go out tonight," I said evenly. "One of my best friends is dead. We just had dinner with her last week. Remember, Rob was there!"

"I was there," Killian remembered. "That was a good night."

"It doesn't seem real that she's gone."

Killian didn't know what to say. "I wish I could tell you something, good, Roddy, but I can't. Look, I'll take you home, but let's sober you up first. Let's get something to eat."

That was fine by me. But Killian wanted to take a tour of Bay Street, the main club area of Staten Island. Bay Street had seen better days. Most of the thoroughfare out ran the gamut through Stapleton, Tompkinsville and St. George. These were neighborhoods that had fallen on hard times, but with the Navy homeport coming in, the Staten Island Chamber of Commerce was banking on better times.

The street was crowded. The night had cleared up and lots of Staten Island youths were out in full force. Rockers frequented their clubs, and guidos did likewise. Rockers and guidos. That was the main rivalry of the day and if you didn't fit in, you were either a.) a preppie, b.) a nerd or c.) a scrub, which I was.

"Some of your shit ilk is out tonight," I mused in disgust.

"Stick it up your ass," came Killian's retort. "Keep it up and you'll be walking home."

Traffic crawled at a slow pace on the thoroughfare. There was something about this scene that struck me as cheap and tawdry. Killian was thinking along the same lines.

"This is a fuckin' joke," chortled Killian. "Look at these sluts walking over here." He gestured to his left at a trio of big-haired bimbos with their breasts practically poking out of their tank tops.

"Hey, look at me!" Killian shouted as he lifted himself off the seat and started to wave his hand up and down toward his crotch area. I started roaring with laughter as he kept on shouting, "Hey, heyyy!" as he alternated propping himself up and waving toward his crotch. That was a pretty amazing feat while he was braking the car.

"Popsicles!" Killian shouted out to the girls. "Get your popsicles here! I'll be the stick; you'll be the pop!"

"Why don't you fuck off, you assholes," one of the girls said angrily.

"Fuckin' blow me, wench, blow me!" Killian shouted back.

"Fuckin' jerk!" the girl shouted back angrily.

"Those girls are begging for it, Roddy; they're friggin' begging for it."

I decided to have my own brand of fun. There was a box of malt balls I had brought at a Manhattan deli. I never got around to eating them and I didn't feel like eating them now. Why not toss these at the freaks walking the street. I tried tossing them at passersby, but I missed.

Killian noticed this and stated, "You really suck. You can't hit any of these people."

"Of course I can't. I'm friggin' drunk."

We were clearing the strip, and there was a cyclist to the right, decked out in his riding gear: the helmet, the reflector around his waist. What an inviting target he made.

I managed to peg him off the helmet. A perfect shot if you ever wanted one.

Those malt balls hurt. I remember some fucktard in one of my classes a couple of years ago hitting me off the back of my head. It felt like a pebble. To this guy, he probably thought it was a rock, because it made a loud pinging sound against his helmet.

"Hey, asshole!" the cyclist shouted. He started pedaling fast to catch up with the car.

"Holy shit, Brian. You'd better burn rubber. I just threw a malt ball at this guy's helmet."

Killian looked through his rearview mirror, and his eyes widened. "Oh, no, you crazy bastard. What the fuck did you do?"

He stepped on the accelerator hard, blowing through the red light we were stopped at and leaving the cyclist behind, shouting and shaking his fist at us.

We arrived at Perkins Cake & Steak on Forest Avenue, which was practically the other side of the Island, 15 minutes later. The place was packed to the gills. Apparently, people coming off the movies or clubbing had the same idea as we both did. There were a few people ahead of us, and wouldn't you know it, Brenda Moriarty was ahead of us on line. She had turned around and noticed me.

"Hey, buddy, small world, isn't it?"

I nodded shyly. There was another girl with her, a brown curly-haired girl about my height, looking like she was in her mid-20s. "Roddy, I would like you to meet my friend Christine. Christine, this young gentleman is Roddy. He's a student of mine."

Christine seemed rather pleasant enough. "Hi, nice to meet you."

I introduced Killian to the ladies. "This is my friend Brian."

Brenda took Killian's hand. "You're the rock star. I heard all about you. Roddy talks about you in his stories."

Killian was perplexed. "Stories?" He eyed me suspiciously. "I hope they're good."

"Don't worry, I won't kiss and tell," Brenda kidded around.

"Funny lady," Killian remarked.

"Would you like to get a table together?" Brenda suggested.

"No, not particularly." I adored Brenda, but I wasn't in the mood for conversing, and I felt uncomfortable with her friend.

"Why, not Roddy?" Killian said. "I want to hear about these stories you have been writing about me." Killian was being a ball breaker, and he was curious about these two beautiful ladies as well as the stories.

All four of us were seated at a table in 10 minutes. Killian and the ladies were gregarious. I was sullen and withdrawn.

"So, what are you boys up to?" Brenda asked.

"Hanging out," I snapped curtly.

"Roddy and I were tearing up the town. This kid is an animal. He got us tossed out of a club — you know The Caves, right?"

"Yeah, where that German restaurant used to be, Demyan's," Brenda chimed in. "I used to eat there a lot with my parents when I was a kid. I'm originally from Stapleton."

"No shit, I live in Clifton on Townsend Avenue by Colonial Lanes. Where in Stapleton?"

"I lived on Van Duzer, before it intersects with St. Pauls Avenue. I live over in Silver Lake now."

"Small world! Anyway, we were at The Caves and Roddy got rowdy. He threw his beer bottle to the floor and started cursing out the joint, calling people assholes. I had to keep the bouncer from throwing his little ass out physically."

"Killian, you are such a fuckin' jerk. Shut up," I bristled in anger.

"Oh my God," Christine laughed. "He looks so young. How does he get into bars?"

"He has a fake ID," Killian explained. "Most of these places don't give a shit. As long as it looks real, they'll let you in."

"Are you serious?" Brenda asked. "Roddy throwing bottles to the floor and cursing out people. That doesn't sound like him."

"Roddy boy is quite rowdy," Killian claimed.

I wished I had a bottle so I could whip it at this Irish sonuvabitch's face. When he drank, he became more gregarious. For me, it all depended on my mood. And my mood was as foul as a skunk at that time, so imbibing in alcohol wasn't the smartest idea I possessed.

"You were no fuckin' choir boy yourself," I spat out. These stories were coming from a man who just recently was lifting himself high in the driver's seat and making hand motions toward his crotch.

The girls were not too fazed. "Boys will be boys," Christine said, utilizing a cliché.

"Tell me, girls, if this kid isn't nuts. He goes to the South Bronx to visit an old friend. I think he's been beaten the shit out of one too many times," Killian volunteered.

"Oh my God," blurted out Christine.

"Roddy, what on earth were you thinking?" Brenda asked in horror. "You could have gotten hurt again or worse. 'Oh my God' is right, Christine."

"None of you would understand it," I proclaimed. I tried telling hair bag this, but it's over his head. It's really no one's business but my own." I looked sharply at a smirking Killian when I said this last part.

The waitress came to take our order. After that, I got up from the table. "Excuse me, but duty calls," I announced as I walked away. I heard Brenda within earshot ask Killian if I was all right.

"He's depressed. Have you heard about the girl who was thrown in front of the subway train?..."

I walked rapidly to the restroom. The beer was working its magic, and Killian's recounting of the tale of Erika started the waterworks. After I finished urinating, I went over to the sink to wash my hands but I fell to the floor, crying and unable to gain the strength to stand.

It was a wave of grief and sadness that wasn't going to leave so quickly. After a couple of minutes, I gathered myself off the tile floor and headed back to the table.

The girls were being regaled by tales from Killian. Christine seemed particularly smitten by him as she glanced at him pie-eyed. Brenda was smiling, but she had the look of "I've heard all this before."

"There he is," Killian proclaimed as I came back to sit down. "We thought you fell in."

Killian was acting like an ass, and I wanted to rap him across the mouth hard, but we had been thrown out of one place already, so why do that again and get these ladies involved?

"You are such a fuckin' idiot sometimes. You really are."

Brenda tried to settle me down. "Take it easy, Roddy. He's only teasing you. Are you feeling okay?"

"No, I'm not okay, but I'll feel better when I get my pancakes."

"Okay, but Brian, take him home after this. He's been through a lot these past few days."

"No problem," Killian answered.

"Roddy, I'm so sorry about your friend," Christine said "I truly am."

I nodded. I appreciated the condolences, but they weren't going to bring my friend back.

Brenda rubbed my shoulder in support. "I know it's hard. There are some real sick people in this world."

Killian, smart guy that he was, changed the subject. "So, what were you ladies up to tonight?"

"Oh, we went to the movies. We saw *The Seventh Sign* with Demi Moore," Christine volunteered. "It wasn't bad."

"It was okay," Brenda chimed in. "Typical horror movie with a bigger budget. I've seen it all before."

"God, you are such a critic, Brenda," Christine chided.

"I've seen better horror movies," Brenda reasoned. "*The Exorcist* scared the shit out of me when I was 14. *The Shining*, that was a real creepy movie. I wouldn't say it scared me like *The Exorcist* did, but you really walked out of that theater unsettled."

"*The Shining* was a great movie," Killian enthused. "Redrum, redrum."

I would have joined the discussion if I was in a better mood. I just wasn't there. I looked away from the group, totally lost in my own thoughts.

"So, tell me something, rock star," Christine asked flirtatiously. "Do you get a lot of girls?"

"No, not at all, Killian said. "I wish I did."

He was such a bullshit artist. "He has a fuckin' girlfriend already," I blurted out. Hell, he had Tabitha. All I got at night in those days were the friggin' sheets.

Killian kicked me hard under the table against my shin. It hurt and I winced. "Asshole, we broke up, remember!" There was a hard look that followed that statement. The snake was trying to get into Christine's pants. Of course he didn't want me to spoil his action. I caught onto his scheme and simply said, "Sorry, I forgot. There were more important things that were happening at the time." I gave Killian a hard look back.

"Oh, I'm sorry to hear that," Christine said. "That must have been tough."

"Yeah, she wasn't around so much anymore. I never got to see her, and it became too difficult."

What horseshit! If I wasn't so depressed, I would have guffawed loudly.

"Well, maybe she was busy but couldn't help it," Brenda offered. "I'm sure she's a college student and she works a lot, am I right?'"

"Yeah," Killian nodded sincerely, "but she wasn't around at all. At least be around some of the time."

"I agree, Christine chimed in. "My ex-boyfriend Danny — he wasn't around in the last two months of our relationship, and then I found out he was going out with this barmaid. Brenda remembers that. She's shared an apartment with me for over two years."

"Yes, I remember that," Brenda said. "You're better off without that loser."

There was a pause in the conversation, and then the food came. I tried tearing through the three-tier level of pancakes as if I were Godzilla tearing through buildings. Killian noticed this since he was sitting directly in front of me.

"Hey, chief, take it easy! You're supposed to eat it, not swallow it." I gather going out had made me a very hungry boy. I did have too much to drink, which was something I normally never had done. I always limited my alcohol consumption to three beers at most. Back at The Caves, I practically drank a whole pitcher by myself, startling Killian.

"Oh, my God, look at him go!" marveled Christine.

"Roddy, easy, hon," Brenda cautioned. "You're going to get sick like that."

I paced myself now that all eyes were looking at me. These people were looking at my every move. "Let me eat in peace, damnit!" my mind screamed.

Killian turned the conversation toward the ladies. "So, how come you two are not taken?" he asked.

"Trying to find a decent guy on this Island is so hard," Christine replied, taking up Killian's challenge.

"Maybe you haven't met the right guy," Killian suggested.

Christine smiled coyly at him, "Ooohh, are you suggesting you're Mr. Right?"

"You never know," Killian answered.

Brenda gave Killian a suspicious smile as if she knew he was full of it. Christine was becoming wide-eyed, taking a strong interest in Killian.

"Why don't we have a double date tonight?" Killian offered. Then he said to Brenda, "Roddy has a crush on you. He always talks about you. 'Brenda this, Brenda that.' He goes on about how you're the best teacher he's ever had. And I didn't believe him when he said that you were pretty, until now. The women teachers I had were dogs."

I was turning colors. If I had a hammer and a set of nails, I would have sealed Killian's mouth shut.

"Aww, he's blushing," Christine cooed.

"Well, thank you, Mr. Rock Star," Brenda said appreciatively. She put her arm around me. "Now, if I was Roddy's age, I would definitely go out with him. He's a sweetheart. But he needs to go out with girls his own age, not an old bag like myself. And you will find that special girl one day, Roddy. I know you will."

It was a truly very generous comment, and Brenda was doing her best to lift my spirits up. Although I wondered if Erika might have been that special girl if I had pursued it. Was Tammy Brascia, Tommasulo's girl, "that special one" that I let get away? Or was this lady next to me the special lady? My confidence level always got an enormous boost from her. With her around, I didn't feel incapable and inept.

After the late-night snack, we all chipped in for the bill. Brenda asked me if I had enough money for my share of the meal, which was very courteous on her part, but I assured her I did. She paid for that lunch back on St. Patrick's Day, so I didn't want to be indebted to her anymore.

I walked away from the booth and found myself tripping onto the carpeted floor. "What the hell?" The first few tables of customers leading from the entrance of the restaurant gaped at my misfortune, while just behind me, to the left, four guidos laughed their asses off about the matter.

"It's really time to get home," I thought. "When you start tripping all over the place, it's time to call it a night."

Brenda approached the table of guidos. "That was really cute," she said to them. "That takes a lot of intelligence. Did you all think of that by yourselves?"

One of them protested to Brenda "We're just foolin' around."

"Oh, really," said Brenda. "Well, then I guess I'm fooling around. She took her right shoe off and slapped the probable perpetrator of tripping me across the head.

"Owww!" yelped the perpetrator in amazement. "What da fuck, lady! Stop!"

After the fourth rap, Brenda stopped. All eyes were on the enraged woman whacking her shoe on this guido's head. Most were quite bewildered. The other three guidos in the booth viewed Brenda with trepidation.

"What's your problem, lady?" the shoe-struck guido bellowed.

"I have a problem with people who pick on my friends," Brenda said calmly but firmly.

"You're lucky I didn't make you eat this fuckin' shoe." She turned away from the group. All the others in the restaurant continued to eye Brenda disbelievingly. I didn't believe this either. Was I hallucinating this whole scenario?

The manager, a white-haired lady came, over distressed. "Young lady, you have to leave now. We can't have this here."

"Don't worry, ma'am, we are leaving," Brenda assured her. She then turned to me to help me off the floor. "C'mon Roddy, let's go home." We exited the restaurant as the hushed crowd looked on.

"That bitch is psycho!" the shoe-clobbered guido declared.

Killian was already at the entrance of the restaurant, having paid the bill. Christine had walked up to the entrance with him. But they had seen the action unfold. Both were horrified at Brenda.

"Brenda, that was insane! What was that all about?" Christine asked in bewilderment.

"That jerk I was hitting with my shoe tripped Roddy over," Brenda bristled with anger as she slipped her shoe back on her foot. He gets picked on so much and without reason. It's pathetic!"

"But you were hitting that guy with your shoe," Christine protested. "Is that how you handle your discipline problems in the classroom?"

"That wasn't class, Christine," Brenda said evenly. "We're not in school, and I'm protecting my friend."

"You're nuts, Brenda," Christine decided. "I could understand you saying something, but you attacked someone with your shoe?"

"You know what, Christine. I don't give a flying fuck."

I was seething with rage. No doubt I was drunk, but I was also well aware of what happened. I pulled out my faux .9 millimeter for all to see.

"I'm gonna do you one better, Brenda. I'm gonna really scare the shit out of them."

To say all three were surprised would be an understatement. They were mortified.

"Tell me I'm not seeing things, Roddy," Brenda asked, trying her best to get to grips with the situation. "That's not real, is it?"

"Oh, my God, oh my God," Christine said over and over again. "This can't be true."

"Holy shit," marveled Killian.

"Why the fuck are you all looking at me like that? You all know how people have fucked with me," I stated. "Do you think I can exist without this?"

Brenda approached me. "Roddy, please talk to me."

"Brenda, just leave me alone, okay. It's a fake gun. It only fires blanks. You'll just tell me how wrong it is to have the gun. Did you know if I didn't have this gun with me, I would have had the shit beat out of me in the Bronx? Three skells tried to take me this morning, but I scared them away."

"Roddy, you'll get into serious trouble if you're caught having this on you," Brenda cautioned. "You could go to jail; and since you are an adult, it would be prison, not some juvenile facility."

"Listen to her, Roddy. She's right," Killian seconded Brenda. "You'll ruin your life if you're caught with that."

I sighed heavily and just sank to the floor, and placed the gun on the ground. I buried my head in my hands and started to break down. Within that moment, Killian came over and kicked the gun away from me.

"I wasn't going to hurt you, Brian," I said, choking back tears. "I wouldn't hurt you, either, Brenda. You two are the only friends I have left."

Brenda knelt beside me and held me. "Brian, give me the gun."

"No, I need that," I cried. "Without that gun, I'm a dead man!"

"Roddy, listen to me. It'll be worse if you don't give it to me." Her blue eyes gazed intently into mine. "Please listen to me."

I knew Brenda had a point, but I didn't want to give up protection. That gun gave me what I needed: security. But the risks were too great, even if it only fired blanks.

"All right, just take it away. I'm fucked no matter what I do."

A wave of nausea gripped me suddenly, and I found myself upchucking my stomach contents all over the ground.

"He's really sick," Brenda exclaimed. "How much did he have to drink, Brian?"

"He had a lot. He practically had a whole pitcher," Killian marveled as if it was some spectacular feat. I guess it was in its unusual way. But it's lame compared to what they do at college campuses nowadays with the 'funneling.'"

A few people walked out of the restaurant and looked at the scene disbelievingly.

"I'm taking him back to our apartment," Brenda said to Christine.

"Why not take him to his own home?" Christine asked in confusion.

"His aunt will kill him," Brenda explained.

"So what? It's his own fault he got drunk. Why should we deal with it?"

"You're not dealing with it, Christine," Brenda stated. "I am."

"It's my apartment too. That impacts me."

"Your apartment? Where was your half of the rent money this month, Christine? You didn't have it, because you're too busy blowing your money on the weekends. Since you didn't pay any of the rent this month and I did, I have the final say."

"Oh my God," Christine said in exasperation. "I do not believe you. You're defending this psycho kid who carries a gun and is puking all over the place because he is drunk beyond belief. He has serious issues."

"Christine, just shut the fuck up," Brenda said in anger. "Just shut the fuck up! He'll sleep on the couch. Why don't you hang out with rock star, err, I mean Brian for awhile. Then you can come back. Just give me an hour to get Roddy situated, okay?"

"Whatever, Brenda. You're just as psychotic as him," Christine declared. Then she turned to Killian. "C'mon rock star, let's hang out for a bit. You can tell me more about yourself."

Killian was stammering; "Oh, okay, but I should really get Roddy home. His…"

"Brian, I'll handle it," Brenda said firmly. "You two just go and have a good time."

Christine shook her head at Brenda. "C'mon, rock star, let's get a cup of coffee someplace." Killian shrugged his shoulders and led Christine to his car.

I was leaning back as Brenda drove, slightly dozing off. "I have to get rid of that gun, Roddy," she said while driving. "What are you thinking, carrying this around? This is so dangerous!"

I was zoning in and out, and the only thing I remember her saying was, "If you feel like you are going to throw up, please throw up into this bag," and she pointed to a plastic shopping bag on the floor by my feet. "Otherwise, you'll be cleaning my car up tomorrow instead of writing."

When I came to her apartment, I woke up and started feeling queasy again. I had just made it up to her toilet in her apartment when I started vomiting again. After standing over me, Brenda put me to bed on the couch. She placed a pail by me.

"Rest up. We'll talk in the morning."

I slept like a baby. My eyes awakened to daylight. The apartment was a two bedroom with a kitchen and living room, and a very spacious one. And it was a homey atmosphere. Magazines and newspapers were piled up on the coffee table. Obviously, Brenda and Christine loved to read. Pictures of Brenda's and Christine's families were scattered about the living room. A large shelf was crammed with books, ranging from Shakespeare classics to modern-day novels.

I turned my attention to the white kitchen. Brenda, clad in black T-shirt, gray sweats and barefoot, was preparing breakfast. She was also wearing round-framed eyeglasses. I had never known her to wear glasses before. And they looked quite flattering on her.

She noticed me getting up. "Good morning. Would you like some breakfast?"

"No, I'd better get going, I said groggily. Surprisingly, my stomach felt a little bit better from the night before. But why chance it?

"Roddy, just have something. You need to eat."

"I've already put you out enough," I said. "I'm trouble and I should get going."

Brenda came over and grabbed me by the hand. "Just come to the kitchen. Please." She escorted me over to the table.

She really cut a sexy figure, even after just rolling out of bed. Damn, she was attractive. I should be lucky one day, I thought, if I could ever have a girl as attractive as this, but also attractive on the inside. She was really sweet and good-natured.

"I only made toast," Brenda said apologetically. "But you really shouldn't eat heavy after last night. How do you feel?"

"I'm okay."

She gave me my plate of two pieces of toast and a glass of apple juice. She then pulled up a chair with a plate of toast for herself and a cup of coffee. "What's up with you, sweetie? Why did you have that gun?"

I sighed and took a deep breath. "I'm friggin scared," Brenda, I confessed. "Someone's going to kill me one day, I just know it."

"Where did you get that gun?"

I went to a gun dealer in the city. He recognized me from the papers. I guess he felt sorry for me, and he sold me a prop gun they use in Hollywood movies. Where's the gun now?"

"I tossed it in the river. If you were caught with that, your life would change and not for the better. It's for your own good."

"How in the hell do I stay safe?" I asked. "Everyone wants to hurt me. It was fake!"

"Roddy, even if it's fake, I don't think you are supposed to have that in the city. It's still illegal."

"It doesn't fire bullets, damnit! It's a blank gun! I'm friggin' dead!"

Brenda exploded. "Jesus Christ, Roddy, will you just shut up and listen to me for one fuckin' minute! You would be in serious trouble if you were caught with that thing. For crying out loud, I'm trying to keep you out of jail. You don't belong there, but if you had tried scaring those guidos in Perkins last night, you would be behind bars now. Maybe I should have let you go in there and get into trouble. Is that what you want?"

"No!" Of course I didn't want that. "I'm just tired of people fucking with me! I've had enough!

There was a pause in conversation for a minute.

"I'm on your side," Brenda said gently. "You don't deserve to be in that kind of trouble, but you have to use your head. If you want to stay safe, stop going into bad neighborhoods and don't travel alone on subways at night!"

I was anguished. "Is it so wrong to visit a person who was once my friend? I just lost a friend, and I have nobody, except Killian."

"No, it's not wrong to visit a friend, Roddy, but you shouldn't go up there alone. You could've asked me to go up there with you. I would have gone, but I would have driven. And I thought I was your friend too. What am I, chopped liver?"

"You're my teacher."

"I think I've become more than a teacher. I'm your friend. But I'm a friend who will always tell you the truth. I will never steer you wrong."

"It doesn't seem real. You're something good that's happening to me, and I don't deserve it. Usually I get bad things happen to me, like getting mugged or one of my friends getting killed."

"You deserve a lot of good things, Roddy." Brenda patted my hand. "I think life will take a better turn for you. Maybe it was just a bad phase you were going through."

"I hope so."

"Things are going to look up for you, hon. I can feel it. Just have faith in yourself, and if you ever need help, never be afraid to ask. Everyone needs help, whether they realize it or not. I had lots of help in my life too."

I could hardly believe that. "You seem so confident and so self-assured. Like you can handle anything."

"It wasn't always that way. And there were times recently where I wasn't confident and self-assured. I just gave a good act."

"Then you should be in Hollywood," I suggested. "You would make a good actress."

"Thank you, that's very sweet of you to say that. But I'm no actress," she laughed." I was never an outgoing person. It was only through teaching I became more outgoing."

"I can't imagine you being shy."

"I was, Roddy. Very shy. I'm pretty sure I told you this already. I had some teachers who were way less than impatient with me.

Like with you, math was a tough subject for me, but the teachers I had were cold, uncaring and they had the attitude if you can't get it right away, they're not responsible. That affected my attitude toward school. But a wonderful teacher named Linda Kaplan, bless her, coached me through life. She was a creative writing teacher in Fort Hamilton High. That woman made me feel so special."

"You told me about her," I reminded Brenda. "It's kind of like you do with me," I pointed out.

"I never thought of me being that way to you, but that's really nice to hear," Brenda said. "Thank you. And you really are one of the best students I ever had."

I shrugged it off. "If you say so."

"Roddy, I know so," she affirmed.

"Did you ever have trouble with the other kids, like I have had?"

"Oh, I had my troubles with the other kids. There were these group of girls that used to taunt me in my freshman year in high school. They were nasty, vicious bitches. They poured milk over me, slapped me, punched me, kicked me on top of the verbal abuse. And in the following year, I shot up in height; when one of those bitches slapped me across the head that first day back, I gave her a beating she never forgot. All three of them were sweet to me as sugar after that."

"It's a shame it has to be that way," I pointed out.

"It is," Brenda concurred, "but that's high school life. You had to find out the hard way like I did." A sudden thought came to me: "Shit, what if my aunt thinks something bad has happened to me? She probably has the cops on the lookout."

"Take it easy, hon, I called your aunt last night. It's all taken care of."

"Well, what did you tell her?" I asked.

"I told her that you and your friend met up with my roommate and me at Perkins. Then we went back to the apartment, we spent all night playing board games and just talking, and then I decided to have you and your friend stay over. Your aunt bought it, and I feel a bit guilty over this, since she seems to think the world of me."

"I wasn't trying to put you out," I said. "I appreciate your covering me."

"You were hurting enough as it is. Your aunt would have given you hell for that, and I could understand that your heart is ripped out after what happened to Erika. I'm angry myself. And I understand why you went up to the Bronx to recapture that friendship with that girl. I only wish you would have called me to take you up there. I know you were depressed and you were drinking heavily because of it. You don't seem to be much of a drinker, right?"

"I like beer, but I usually am limited to two."

"Just don't ever let drinking get out of control like it did with me."

I was startled by that statement. "You?"

Brenda nodded sheepishly. "Yes, I'm not exactly a sterling role model, and I can't lecture you on how you shouldn't be drinking. But I can tell you that if you let any drug get a hold of you, it could ruin your life. Three years ago, I discovered to my horror that my joint bank account I shared with my husband was wiped out of savings. He had developed a cocaine habit, and it had been going on for a while. But I was so consumed with school and my career, I never saw it. All right, I was furious, but the man had a problem, and I did marry him. I made that vow to take care of him through sickness and in health. Any addiction is a sickness. I would get him through that."

She sucked her breath in hard before she went on. "Then I caught the bastard cheating in our own house with his secretary. He owned a plumbing business, which is why he had that slut around. I got a hold of a frying pan, and I chased him and that bitch out of the house. I was so livid, I could have committed murder if I had connected with my swings."

I sat there taking it all in, blown away by these details.

"The divorce was messy, as you can imagine. I was broke as a result, because whatever funds my husband earned with his plumbing business, he snorted away. Mine as well. I wound up living at home with my mom before I could get back on my feet. Unfortunately, I started drinking heavily. It all came to a head when I crashed my car into a barrier. I wrecked the car and was lucky to walk away. I knew right then and there I needed help, so I decided to make a concerted effort never to have another drop of alcohol. I've been sober for over a year now, but once an alcoholic, always an alcoholic. "I'm just a recovering one."

"That's quite a story," I remarked. "I'm really sorry to hear about all of that, but I don't get your ex-husband. Any guy would be lucky to have you as a wife."

"I don't get men at all," Brenda stated. "Ever since the divorce, I haven't gone out with another man. I prefer the company of women nowadays."

My ears perked up. "You mean you're gay?" I asked in amazement.

Brenda nodded affirmatively.

I was taken aback by this revelation. "Are you and Christine?..."

"We have been intimate, but she prefers the company of men more."

"Holy shit," I muttered to myself, stupefied.

"Well, I can see this news has taken you quite by surprise," Brenda joked. "I hope this doesn't change things between you and me."

"No way." I was never expecting it. "I don't think any less of you. You're a hero to me."

"You are way too sweet. I'm not a hero. I'm just an ordinary person who has her problems and quirks." Then Brenda added seriously, while touching my hand, "Thanks for accepting me for that, Roddy. Not too many people would."

I had been judged quite enough by people. I didn't give a damn about her sexual preferences; Brenda was fantastic to me. Very few people ever respected me back then, and here was someone who treated me as if I counted for something. I would go through a brick wall for her, and if anyone tried to hurt her, I would kill them.

"Thank you, dear."

Brenda mentioned something about her mom, and I asked her if both her parents were living still. "No," Brenda stated, "my father was killed in a construction accident when I was only 17. He slipped and fell five stories from a building he was working on in Manhattan. My mom lives down in Florida."

"I'm sorry about your dad."

"Thanks. I was really devastated at the time. My mom, especially. But now it seems like ages. You never get over it, but the more time goes by, it's a bit easier to deal with."

I brought up Liz Cartegna, the lady who had offered to help me find Jasmine. Brenda remembered her well. "Liz is a nice person. She has a great sense of humor. She had me rolling in that writing class, and I loved her tales of Highbridge. If a person can survive growing up there, that person can survive anything."

I complimented Brenda on her eyeglass wear.

"Roddy, you are so kind to me, thanks. I'm short-sighted, so I usually wear contacts all the time. I'm self-conscious with the way I look in glasses."

"You shouldn't be embarrassed. It's a great look on you. Why don't you wear them to the park today?"

She mulled that over. "You know, I'm awfully tired of placing these contacts in my eyes all the time. What the hell, why not?"

After a few minutes more in her apartment, I decided that I had worn out my welcome. "I better get on home. Thanks for putting up with me."

"Roddy, you have a class with me today, remember?"

"I'm not up to it, Brenda. Besides, I don't have the assignment I did."

"Why not do it here? I'll give you a pen and some paper; it's no big deal. Besides, it would do you good to be with friends today. You shouldn't be alone."

That was true. And while I still felt depressed by Erika's death, I was able to feel better by being with friends.

And once again, Brenda saved my life.

We were crossing Victory Boulevard into Silver Lake Park. I had stepped into the road, and a Corvette came racing up the boulevard. Brenda pulled me out of the way of that speeding car. Partly it was my fault. I wasn't paying close attention, still dwelling about Erika's death. But that driver was doing at least 60 in a 35 mph zone.

"What an asshole," Brenda muttered about the driver. "Roddy, you really have to be careful crossing here. They drive crazy on the Island anymore."

It was a good day for a writing session. The rest of the class was complimentary on Brenda's glasses, and it made me feel really good to see her encouraged by the class. She was always encouraging all of us; why couldn't we give her a little something back. I found it strange with this seemingly self- confident person that she would be self-conscious about wearing glasses.

I felt bad for Tim, who continued to write about his stuttering problems. He was a freshman at St. Peter's Catholic School, and was taking heavy taunting from the other students. I wished I could go there and help straighten out those wise-ass bastards for him.

Brenda was instructing him gently: "Try to relax before you speak. Take your time in speaking. Your confidence will build up that way. The ones who care about you will understand."

It was really a touching scene. There was no doubt Brenda had her flaws; she had a trigger-haired temper as witnessed by that restaurant episode, and she was a recovering alcoholic. But her heart was huge. She invested her own time with the four of us even when she wasn't getting paid. How many people do you know who would do that?

More Bumps in the Road

The wake came and went for Erika. I attended but could only stay 10 minutes. It was a closed-casket affair. God knows what she looked like! I paid my respects to her parents and her younger sister, who were obviously and understandably distraught. That was just a bad scene. It brought back home to me what had happened with Uncle Harry a year earlier. Saying "sorry" could never be enough. It was so trite. How could it possibly bring their daughter back?

Brenda had stated that Sunday morning that my life would get better. Well, it sure as hell didn't feel like it was. On that following Saturday night after work, I met up with Killian, and we attended the NY Auto Show at the old New York Coliseum in the Hell's Kitchen area of New York, infamous for the Westies gang and now undergoing gentrification. It was a big rip off as far as I was concerned. You pay $15 to see automobiles that you could very well see in a showroom, and you could get the brochures at any auto dealership. What a lame scene that was. Before we left, I made a trip to the bathroom.

There was a short guy, dark skinned, with a pencil-thin mustache and dressed in gray work clothes, inside the bathroom. I guess he was the janitor. He walked by me as I headed for the stall and felt my crotch area in a quick, blink-or-you'll-miss moment. I was not sure if I had felt that or was imagining things. I proceeded to the stall, and the janitor walked out of the bathroom. After I walked out of the bathroom, the janitor passed by me again and copped another feel. I knew that time that I wasn't imagining things. I made a grab for his head and rammed it through the bathroom door, propelling both of us inside the bathroom. I followed up with a knee smash to his face, and I noticed blood spurting out of his nose. The blood didn't stop me from wanting to pulverize the perverted bastard even more. When he fell to the ground, I didn't let up my attack. My legs started swinging at his body. I wanted to kick the shit out of this pustule into oblivion. He was moaning, "No, no, n—nn-no." His moans did not deter me as I stomped on the man's right hand, the same hand he had felt my crotch with. If I could chop it off, I would have gladly done so, but I had no cutting device. The best thing I can do was break it, which is what I was aiming for. He let out more moans as I continued to stomp on his hand, now turned to mush. My anger was still running high as I took the towel dispenser off its hinges and bounced it off his head for good measure. He lay there unconscious. I quickly left the bathroom and caught up with Killian, who was waiting by the front entrance.

"Let's get the fuck out of here, fast!"

"We are, man," Killian said.

"Let's fuckin' boogie!" I certainly wasn't talking about disco dancing.

"What's going on with you?" Killian demanded. "It looks like you've seen a ghost."

"Worse, man, they have a janitor here who felt my crotch," I explained as we walked out into the lobby area of the coliseum. My hands were bloodied, and I was doing my best to conceal them in my pockets so the front security guard wouldn't notice them.

"What!" Killian looked at me disbelievingly. "Are you serious?"

"Of course I'm serious! I just gave him a massive beating in the bathroom."

"Roddy, what the fuck are you talking about?"

"There's a perverted fuck in there who felt my crotch area when I came into the bathroom. I just gave him a fuckin beating. I smashed his head against the sink and I kicked him all over the place. He's a mess in there. Can't you see the blood on my hands?" I took a hand out of my pocket to show him the blood. "How fuckin' dense are you, Brian? Let's get the fuck out of here already!"

"'Jesus Christ, hanging out with you is an adventure, man, an adventure," Killian said.

We got on the nearest subway train heading for South Ferry. It took me 20 minutes to calm down, in which time we made our connection at the ferry terminal. Killian all the while was doing his best to relax me. I did what I could to wipe the blood off my hands with a handkerchief, so no one would be the wiser.

"Take it easy, man. The asshole had it coming. I would have done the same thing. Nobody's going to find out nothing — nobody will know."

"Shut the fuck up," I rasped. "Keep your mouth shut." Part of me wondered if all that guitar distortion was chipping away at Killian's brain.

"Let's get a few beers at the bowling alley," Killian suggested.

We got to Killian's house on the border of the Rosebank/ Clifton section of the Island. I washed the blood off my hands, and we proceeded down his street, Townsend Avenue, to the old Colonial Lanes, probably the oldest bowling alley on the Island. Both of us sat at a table and talked over a couple of beers.

"That teacher of yours is hot," Killian commented. "I'd do her in a second."

I bristled with anger at Killian. Wasn't this hound getting enough between two women? And the thought of Killian going out with Brenda. That was a disgusting thought. "Hey, keep your dick away from her! She's not for you!"

Killian was taken aback by my reaction. "Take it easy, psycho. I wasn't planning to go near her. I'm fucking her friend, Christine, right now, and it is the best sex I've ever had. That night we left you and Brenda, we fucked right in the back seat of the car. That chick was like the Energizer bunny. She kept going and going and..."

"...Give me a fuckin' break, already. So Christine is a fuck machine. But she's not a particularly nice person. I heard some of the things she said about me last week. That I'm a 'psycho.' Let's see her go through the shit I went through lately."

"No, she understands it now. I told her all about you. She felt really bad."

"Do me a favor don't tell anybody about me, okay?" I requested. "I don't need anyone's sympathy."

I decided to bring up a new subject. "What about Tabitha?"

"What about her?" Killian asked.

"You're still going out with her, pinhead, right?"

"Yeah, I'm still going out with her."

"But what are you planning to do? You can't keep both of them."

"Why not? They don't have to know," Killian said in a matter-of-fact fashion.

"Does Christine know you have a girlfriend?"

"I think she does, but I don't think she cares."

"And Tabitha doesn't know?"

"No, she doesn't," Killian responded testily. "What the hell do you care?"

"I just think Tabitha is a nice person. I wish she was my girlfriend."

"Yeah, she's nice, but I'm only 20 years old, Roddy. I'm too young to get tied down with a chick. Why not play the field for a while? Besides, Christine is better in bed than Tabitha. It was the best sex I've ever had, and Tabitha has been too busy lately. Why can't she be there when I need her?"

"C'mon, you know she goes to school. She can't help that. And she works too."

"I know, I know," said Killian sheepishly, "but Christine is so different. When we had sex, there were sparks shooting off us. Really, electric sparks!"

Christine was a pretty girl, no doubt about it, and I'm sure Killian was telling me the truth. Still and all, I didn't much like her, and Tabitha was always nice to me. But was it really my business?"

"That teacher of yours is nuts about you," Killian declared. "She really likes you."

"Not that way," I countered.

"I don't know; anyone who throws a shoe at a guido who tripped you over has to have something for you."

"Let's not get overboard, man. She likes me; she doesn't love me."

"Are you kidding me? She thinks you're cute, and she said she'd go out with you if she were your age."

"Yeah, my age, but she's not. She's older than me."

"It doesn't matter. You should tell her you love her."

"I'm 17; she's 29 years old. Couldn't she get into trouble? Isn't that statutory rape?"

"No, 17 is legal, man. It's a legal age. She can fuck you without getting into trouble."

"I think you're wrong on that."

"I don't think I am."

"You're getting crazy, man. It's not happening. I like her and that's it. She's hot, but I'm not interested in her in that way."

"Roddy, don't bullshit me. I never heard you talk about a girl before. I wondered at times if you were a fag. I mean, I'm glad you talked about that chick Jasmine, and that you have the hots for your teacher. I used to point out hot babes and you never used to get excited."

"I was looking for the right girl. But the girl I like is too old. And so what — what if I *was* gay," I bristled. "You would drop me like a hot potato?"

"No way. But it would make things a bit uncomfortable. What if you really were secretly in love with me?"

"Don't delude yourself, you fuckin' pinhead. There are lots of guys out there who are far better looking than you, and I don't have to be gay to say that."

"Ahhh, fuck you!"

"Look, it's never going to happen with Brenda. That would be great, but let's get real here. There's too much of an age difference, and I'm still technically a kid!"

"That's too bad; I'd be on her like white on rice."

"I'm sure you would. You're a fuckin' snake, but if you tried anything, she'd kick your balls in." I wondered if I should let on that Brenda was a lesbian. But it wasn't my place to divulge that information. Would Brenda want that information out? How many people knew besides Christine? Still, it would have been interesting to get Killian's reaction.

"Yeah, she is nuts. But that was funny when she was hitting that gueed over the head with her shoe."

"I didn't expect that, either. But she's the best teacher I ever had, Brian. She actually gives a shit. I had too many teachers who never cared."

"So did I. And if she really helps you that way, that's cool."

There was a pause in the conversation as we saw a couple of guidos and their girlfriends waltz into the bar area. The guidettes were smoking hot. At my age, my hormones were especially raging. But I knew these girls wouldn't give me the time of day.

Killian turned the conversation to my future plans. "So, what are you planning to do after graduation?"

"I have no idea."

"You don't know? What about this film school you were talking about?"

"Do you know how much money that shit costs? My aunt can never afford that!"

"Then why don't you move out to Hollywood? Try applying to a studio. Get a job as a gopher. Work your way up the ladder."

"That's an idea. But I would really have to save up more money before I could move out there."

"When am I going to see more of your writing?" Killian demanded. "All I saw was that teenage *Death Wish* screenplay. It was good, but vigilante movies have been done to death. Come up with something new!"

Our conversation was distracted when one of the guidettes dropped her pocketbook and bent ass over to pick it up.

"Oh, shit, look at that," Killian whispered.

I looked briefly. The girl was hot with teased big hair, a beautiful Italian olive skin complexion, a pink tank top and sweatpants that were tight on her, just coming above her bare ankles. Killian muttered a low "Wow." I looked briefly but didn't want to a make it so obvious. One of the guidos was big and chunky. If he caught us looking at his girl, he'd rip our faces off.

As luck would have it in little Roddy's world, the big gueed noticed us taking a gander at his girl's ass. He was none too happy about it.

"What da fuck youse clowns looking at?"

Killian, smart ass that he was, wasn't at a loss for words. "I'm looking at your girlfriend — what do you think I'm looking at?"

"Oh, you think you're being funny, dirtbag? It won't be funny when my fist connects with ya face."

"Hold, on," Killian quickly interjected. "There's no need for violence. I'm a guy, my friend is a guy. It's natural to look at girls.

What do you expect us to look at, guys? We can't help it if your girl is hot and has a big ass!"

My face fell. "Killian, you idiot."

The gueed was too shocked to react. He was not the sharpest pencil in the box, so he couldn't form a quick reaction to Killian's compliment, or insult, depending on the way you looked at it.

Killian took the pitcher of beer and poured it over the gueed's head. I was stunned by my friend's actions, as was the gueed and his friend.

Killian pulled me out me out of the chair. "Let's get the fuck outta here!"

We ran out of the bowling alley with the beer-soaked gueed and his friend, a medium-sized guy, hot on our tails. Killian and I were the faster sprinters, but the gueeds could hold their own.

Beer-soaked gueed could move surprisingly fast for a guy who was heavy.

"Head for the fuckin' train!" Killian cried out. "The fuckin' train!" Above us was the Clifton train station. We heard the rumble and the screeching of brakes of the Staten Island Rapid Transit bound for Tottenville, the last outpost on Staten Island.

We ran out onto Bay Street. My mind questioned why this nut job was heading for the train. But I just kept running and placed my faith in Killian's hands.

We would have done Jesse Owens proud as we raced up those stairs. The train had stopped, and its doors were already opened as Killian and I raced down the platform toward the front car. We didn't look back to see if our pursuers were on our tail. We just concentrated on getting on that first car. And by pure chance, we just managed to get on before the doors closed, and we found ourselves heading off toward the southerly direction of Staten Island.

Killian and I looked around the train nervously to see if we truly had eluded our pursuers. The only other person on board was a man in his 50s reading the *New York Post*.

"Did we lose these clowns?" I asked Killian in desperation.

"I don't see them," he answered.

"What the fuck is wrong with you, man?" I demanded. "Pouring beer over that guido's head!"

"He's a dumb fuck," Killian interjected. Then he launched into an imitation of the guido. "'You're looking at my girl's ass.' Did you see her ass? She was hot!"

"Yeah, I saw that. But do you have to be friggin' blatant about it? And what is that shit with the beer over his head?"

"Oh, fuck him. He's a dumb shit. Maybe that beer will soak into his head, wake up a few dead brain cells."

I laughed but only for those brief few seconds. The lumbering behemoth and his sidekick were coming our way. They had made their way by crossing through the cars of the train. Obviously, they weren't that stupid and were smart enough to find the asses they wanted to kick the shit out of. The asses of Killian and myself.

I noticed them before my laughing counterpart, who was priding himself on his wit and humor.

"Oh, no. We're dead," I said, eyeing the bullish guido, still soaked from the beer, eyes slits of anger, hell-bent on kicking some ass. I can't say I blamed the guy after getting doused with beer.

"You assholes are dead! Dead!" shouted the big kid.

There was nowhere to run, no escape hatch. I had no choice but to stand my ground and get the shit kicked out me along with my counterpart. My fake gun was floating someplace in New York harbor, thanks to Brenda, and now I wish she hadn't done that. At least it would have scared them off. All I had for protection was a Swiss army knife. Killian carried a commando knife made popular by those *Rambo* movies, but I seriously wondered if he would ever use it. Unlike me, he was pretty handy with his fists. I have seen him take on three guys at once out on the street, tossing one kid head-first into a car bumper. The second, he gave a nice well-placed punch to the throat, practically knocking that kid to the ground, wheezing for air. And the third kid, he kicked hard in the solar plexus. I had thought I was viewing an action movie. And how could I forget the fight with Rossi?

Now I was preparing to be a dead man, and I was wondering if Killian could fight his way out of this one. Before I could get that answer, I heard a voice yelling behind the oncoming duo.

"Hey! Don't you fuckin' guys listen? How about paying your goddamn fare! Pay it now, or I'll toss both of yas off this train. I'm not fuckin' kidding."

The conductor, a tough-looking Italian guy, in his 30s, was heading toward the duo. He looked like a person who didn't mess around and could handle himself.

The big, burly guido turned around to face the conductor and yelled out, "Fuck you!"

"You're a wise ass, you fuckin' piece of shit, aren't ya?" the conductor snarled, still rushing up toward them. He slapped the big gueed hard across his head.

"Hey," sputtered the big gueed. "Whadda fuck?"

The conductor followed up with another hard smack to the gueed's head. "Ya think ya tough, asshole, huh?" This question was punctuated by another smack to the big gueed's head. "Leave me the fuck alone, man," the gueed whimpered. His counterpart looked on in horror.

"Ya think you can wise off to me, huh, ignore me! Well, you and your friend are getting off this train, and if you give me anymore shit, I'll beat the fuck out of you and your pussy friend. Ya got it?"

Another hard smack followed when the big gueed didn't answer right away. "Ya fuckin' got it, you fat piece of shit?"

The big gueed was cowering, and the conductor was only a couple of inches taller than I am, whereas the gueed towered at 6 foot 2.

"All right, man, we're getting off!" the big gueed yelled back in fear, not wanting to get another slap across the head.

The wiry gueed, who looked like a horse with the ridiculous mullet of a crewcut hairstyle on top with long hair curling past the collar, tried to speak up. "But Mista. These two threw beer at my friend, and we were..."

"...Shut up. Just shut up," the conductor interrupted. "Both of youse. Two fuckin' dickhead drunks who get on my fuckin' train. Now, you get ya asses off at the next stop: Grasmere!"

"Wait a minute, will ya!" yelled the big gueed in protest. "We were chasing these guys and..."

"...I don't give a shit," the conductor interrupted. "Next time you come aboard here, try to drink your beer, not wear it."

"But what about those guys? Aren't you going to ask them if they paid their fare?"

That was the wrong question to ask the conductor. "Are you trying to tell me how to do my job, ya pinhead, because I'll pinch your head off like a grape. The train is pulling in right now, so youse guys get off."

The big gueed turned to both of us before getting off the train, and said, "You're dead, both yas. I'll fuckin' find yas, you can count on it." They both stepped off into the night. And the doors closed behind them. The conductor turned his attention to us. "I hope youse guys have the fare."

We had to get off anyways, which we did at the next stop: Old Town. This was an area I was not very familiar with, but it seemed like a nice enough area. Killian knew it: "I used to date a girl who lived around here," he reminisced. "I think the street was Providence."

"Who cares what girl you banged? How the hell do we get back?"

"We can't take the train. Those guys will be waiting for us in Grasmere. So we're better off taking the bus."

"What's the matter? You're scared of that guido? Are you afraid he'll kick your ass in?"

"Fuck no! And be lucky I don't kick your ass in for even suggesting that!" was my friend's retort to my sarcastic query. I was only too glad to get home, and I'm sure Killian was as well. What a wild, weird and interesting night. Not the kind of night one would have liked to have all the time, and I could have done without that perverted bastard in the bathroom at the auto show.

My First Documentary

Brenda prodded me to film the class, and on that Sunday before Memorial Day, I did just that with my camcorder. Timmy was very reluctant to speak in front of the camera, so Brenda arranged for him to speak off a cue card he wrote for himself:

"Hi, my name is Tim Hinton. I'm a sophomore high school student at St. Peter's High School, and this class means a lot to me. I'm getting personal instruction from a teacher who's the best I ever had, Brenda Moriarty. Brenda tells me I express myself in words, and she's encouraging me to write more. I hope to be a writer one day."

We all had our personal interviews with the camera, myself included. Brenda held the camera for me during my interview:

"Hi, my name is Roddy McPherson, and I'm soon to be a high school graduate, I hope. This writer's workshop has been a great help to me. It's given me more confidence in myself as a person and as a writer. I hope to make a career out of writing, preferably screenplays. And the teacher, Brenda Moriarty, is the greatest ever. No teacher I've ever had has been as encouraging as she has been."

Latiesha: "Hi, my name is Latiesha Wilkins, and I'm a graduating senior at Normand High. The class has helped my writing a lot, but what I like more than the class is the teacher, Brenda Moriarty. Not many teachers understand kids, but Ms. Moriarty does. I want to be the kind of teacher Ms. Moriarty is."

Lucia: "Hi, my name is Lucia Sanchez. I'm a junior at Curtis High School. I don't know what I want to do with my future yet. I do know I wish to work with kids, and I hope to be the kind of person Brenda is. My home life isn't the best. The class is an escape for me, and the teacher provides a home for me that's better than my real home..."

Lucia started to cry uncontrollably. Brenda had to take her to the side and comfort her.

I saved our peerless leader for last: "Hi, my name is Brenda Moriarty, and I'm the teacher of this writer's workshop. Each of these kids is very special and they are all talented. But unfortunately, they have had difficult home lives and difficult circumstances that have happened to them. When you have terrible circumstances in life, it tends to take your focus away from learning and it can affect your self-confidence. Each of these kids is a gifted writer, and they all come from different backgrounds. I have no doubt they will triumph over the adversity they face, but everyone needs help, and if I can provide a positive atmosphere where they can have enjoy themselves and enrich their knowledge, that means a lot to me. I didn't intend it as a home away from home for these kids, but it just happened that way. And if it helps their self-esteem, then I can't complain about it. I'm actually thrilled!"

I took video footage of the students while they read their work. None of them had any problem with me filming the class, and they all wished to see the final product. Brenda offered to have us view the finished product in her apartment the following week.

I had forgotten my jacket in Brenda's apartment, so I had to go back with her to get it.

While in the apartment, I asked her if she wanted to add more to her interview. She readily agreed:

Q: What inspired you for the idea for the writer's workshop?
A: I saw the potential that some kids had when it came to writing. As you know, I teach a creative writing class at Normand High School. And there are some kids who are quite creative. I felt that as much as I try to make the class educational and fun, it just isn't enough for some students who are quite talented with their writing. They need more. So why not have an afterschool workshop? When I suggested the idea to the administration of the school, they felt there wouldn't be enough interest in the class. But I still wanted to get something going, so I decided to get a few select kids together, and provide a small, unofficial workshop for them. The kids in this workshop are quite talented writers, but they have faced a lot of hardships in their lives, and they need an escape. It wasn't intended that way, but I guess it's become like that.

Q: Can anyone join this workshop?

A: I tried passing word in my classes, but most are not interested. Most of them may work, or they might have school work that takes up their time. Other kids visit family, or maybe they just want to hang out. Sunday is an odd day to hold a workshop, but it was the only day anyone could agree on.

Q: And it's true you don't get paid for your time?

A: No, I don't.

Q: Then why go through the trouble?

A: It's no trouble at all. I love doing this, and I even participate myself. It's a release for me too, and I genuinely like the kids. They really are good kids, and for them it's a big thing. I'm not looking to make a profit out of this. My biggest payback is helping kids, and when you see how receptive they are, that makes it all worthwhile.

Q: Do you enjoy teaching?

A: I love it. I couldn't imagine myself doing anything else. I love working with kids, and in my classes I have a good rapport.

Q: Did you ever have any disciplinary problems?

A: Of course. Every teacher has had them. There's that incident that happened in Brooklyn where two boys got into a fight and one of them fell out of a window sill. That happened in my class, and that's something I'd just rather forget. But these things do happen, unfortunately. Usually, a discipline problem may involve an unruly or talkative student. You have to maintain a tough front and be firm; otherwise, you'll get taken advantage of.

Q: Tell me about the students in your writer's workshop class.

A: Well, I have four. There's Latiesha. She's a senior and her writing is really descriptive, almost as if she is painting a picture. And since she lives in Park Hill, which is one of the tougher neighborhoods on Staten Island, she has some harrowing tales, which makes my hair stand up on end even without the mousse. But she really is a fighter, very streetwise and tough. She aspires to be a teacher, and with that level head on her shoulders, she'll make it. Than we have Lucia, a really sweet girl. She's a sophomore and she writes really beautiful poetry. Sometimes a harrowing poem may slip through, and it's understandable with domestic abuse existing in that household. I worry about her in that environment, and I have tried from my end to help. I don't know if I'll be successful. Lucia aspires to be a social worker and fortunately, or unfortunately, she has great experience already.

We have Timmy, or Tim, as he prefers to be called. He's a sophomore like Lucia. He has a stuttering problem, and it's heart-wrenching to see, but you wouldn't know it from his writing. His command of the language is impressive. He will make a superb writer one day, but that taunting he takes over his stuttering is just so hard to hear about. You just hope his self-confidence never wavers.

And last but not least, we have Roddy. What a roller coaster ride Roddy has been through this semester! A mugging, getting involved in two armed robberies, one in which he was hurt, and the other where he subdued an armed gunman. And there was the murder of one of his best friends recently. It's amazing how he has not cracked under all of this. He came close, but he held together. But he escapes like the others through his writing. Roddy is the least technically polished out of my writers in the workshop, but raw, gritty emotionalism pushes him right through. The energy is startling. There is a lot of talent there. He states that he wants to be a screenwriter, but he's better off writing short stories or novels. His writing is too good for making blueprints of movies. But it's his life, and he's had a problem with self-esteem, but he's gotten better. Everyone has a personal favorite in classes, and I would have to choose him.

Brenda then added with a wink: "Don't tell anyone, Roddy. You'd better edit that out."

Q: Would you encourage writing as a career for these students?

A: Only if they really wanted it. But they would have to get something concrete in their lives to fall back on. Latiesha plans to be a teacher, so that's a good career choice to make. Maybe I'm biased, but it's true. Lucia uses her writing as an outlet, but she plans to be a social worker. Since Tim is a sophomore, it's kind of early to recommend a career path for him And Roddy wants to get involved in Hollywood, one of the more difficult career moves. I wouldn't recommend writing on its own, because it's not a stable career. There's a lot of rejection and even if you happen to get published, you're not guaranteed to sell. You have to have a stable career to fall back on. Personally, I'd rather eat than starve."

Q: A final question: Have you ever been published?
A: I submitted short stories to magazines, and I've won some prizes. It's no big deal. I was working on a novel, but I got sidetracked with further schooling I'm undergoing as of now. But perhaps one day.

The interview ended. Brenda was amazed. "Those were really good questions, hon! Oh my God, you could be a journalist! Forget Hollywood!"

"Film is where I want to be," I said. "I wish I could go to film school, but my aunt won't go for it. So I might as well go to Hollywood."

"It's going to be expensive living out there, even more so than New York," Brenda pointed out.

"I don't know what else I would like to do."

"Go find a community college that has a good film studies program. Minor in that, but major in something concrete. Be a journalist or a teacher."

I just sighed. "You grownups have no clue about me."

"Oh, give me a break, Roddy. I have gotten to know you well in these past five months. I'm trying to give you good advice. I know your strong suit is writing, and you should do something in that vein. Would I ever steer you wrong?"

"No, you never did."

Christine came bouncing into the apartment, dressed up in a pink exercise tank top, pink shorts, white headband and sweat glistening off her tanned body She was bouncy and cheery. "Hey

Brenda. Roddy, hello! How are ya?" What a change from the previous week and her attitude toward me. I simply nodded at her. She
seemed friendly now.

"So what are you guys doing?" she asked, genuinely interested.

"Roddy was interviewing me. He's making a documentary of
the workshop."

"Oh, that is really cool. I'd like to see it," Christine further
enthused. "Excuse me, I'll be right back; I have to go to the
bathroom."

"Last week she couldn't stand me; now she's interested in what
I do?" I wondered aloud to Brenda.

"I explained it all to her about you," Brenda replied.

"So did Killian. I don't want people feeling sorry for me."

"After people hear your tales of the last five months, how can
they not?" Brenda reasoned. "I had to explain to her why I had
displaced her out of the apartment for the night. I was pretty harsh
with her, but she didn't mind too much. She hit it off with your
friend Brian."

"Yeah, she sure did," I mused.

"I didn't believe a word he said about him breaking up with his
girlfriend. She's still seeing him, isn't she?" Brenda asked.

I gave Brenda a sick look. "What do you think?"

"I suggested to Christine that he may be still involved. But she
doesn't care. She tells me it's the hottest sex she ever had. That girl
is impulsive when it comes to men. Unbelievable! It's my fault for
suggesting they go someplace that night!

"Isn't that my fault?" I reasoned.

"Please stop blaming yourself, Roddy for things that are not
your fault. You're too hard on yourself as it is, and that hurts me."

"I don't want to be a snitch and tell his girlfriend."

"Don't bother. He'll get caught himself. Guys who are that arrogant usually do."

I felt bad for Tabitha most of all, but it wasn't my business.
Besides, I had my own problems to deal with.

You Can't Win 'Em All

Even though I was a senior, I was not getting off scot free from the abuse of cretins. There were various gym classes changing in the locker room. One maggot feasted his eyes on me, a Korean kid named Ki-wan. He was about my height, very stylish looking with his spiky mullet. I don't know what it was, but the Asians wore that spiked hair style best. Perhaps because their hair was straight and naturally suited for that style. But good hairstyle or not, the kid was a prick and took it upon himself to antagonize me for no reason.

"Hey," he called out of the blue one particularly hot June day. "Do you ever talk?"

What a stupid ass question! "When I want to," I answered simply.

"Do you ever curse?" Ki-wan asked again.

"Yeah, I curse. Why?"

"I don't believe it. You look like a mama's boy to me. Say 'motherfucker.'"

Ki-wan was just your typical parasite at school, trying to assert himself over a person he thought weak. The last six months had not been kind to me and they did not make me a gentleman, especially when dealing with a hunk of shit like this kid. I immediately went for his shirt lapels and backed the surprised and suddenly terrified tormentor against his opened locker door.

With the other hand, I grabbed the kid by his spiked hair and banged his head hard against his locker door.

"Let me go, man, get the fuck off!" he wailed.

"Stay the fuck away from me, you piece of shit. Just stay the fuck away or your head will be part of this locker." I bashed his head against the door for good measure.

He didn't say anything, so I bashed his head against the door again. "Did you hear me, you sonuvabitch? Fuckin' answer me!"

"Yeah, I heard ya. Get off me! Just get off!"

"Don't fuck with me," I snarled. "When you see me, you don't even speak to me." I placed my right hand against his neck, choking him. His brown skin was turning red, and he was gagging.

"Don't fuck around or I'll kill you," I threatened. I released my choke hold, leaving Ki-wan slumping to the ground and gasping for air.

"Did you fuckin' hear me?" I rasped in a snarl. Ki-wan looked at me warily and nodded yes.

I had survived a mugging and two robberies. Ki-wan was an inconsequential pustule compared with all that. I would have been out of my mind to take his shit, especially at that juncture.

A few rubberheads saw the action and gawked at us, as if they had never seen a fight in their lives. I tried to pay them no mind. It was June and I wanted this nightmare of a semester to be over.

But rather than feel at ease after knocking Ki-wan's head into the locker, I was really upset about it. I was close to 18 years old. At that point in time, why on earth did I have to fight anyone at all? I ruminated on the prior events through my next two classes. Good-natured Brenda noticed my downcast demeanor throughout the class. After the bell rang, she stopped me.

"What's going on with you, Roddy?"

"Nothing at all."

"You can't fool me, Roddy. Your facial expressions are so readable. I can tell when something is bothering you."

I sighed. "I really don't want to talk about it, if you don't mind."

"I bet you got into it with another student, right?"

"How the hell did you know?" I wondered in amazement.

"Aside from Erika's death, your main issues this year have been concerning a teacher or another student. That's when you seem to be the most visibly upset."

I sucked in my breath hard. I told her about Ki-wan and how I nipped that problem in the bud. Brenda merely shook her head.

"Listen, Roddy, try to back off from fighting. Graduation is in a few weeks. Just walk away from the fights. It's not worth getting suspended when the finish line is so near."

"I would love to, but these punks make it so hard."

"Ignore it hon; you're almost out of here."

"Easier said than done," I said to myself as I exited the classroom. Ki-wan was subdued the next day and just nodded to me. Obviously, our little discussion worked, but a new problem appeared. A big kid by the name of Marty Flanagan, a senior, came over to me. He was in the regular gym class like Ki-wan was, and I wondered why he was approaching me.

"Hey, you're name is McPherson, right?"

"Yeah."

"You're a tough guy, right?"

"When I have to be," I simply replied. I didn't like where this was headed.

"So, you think you're tough?" Flanagan persisted.

I was getting exasperated. "What do you want?"

"I hear you're a tough guy, that you beat the shit out of some kid on the football team, and that you bashed a kid's head into a locker."

This kid was checking me out to see if I would fight him; I simply turned away from him and stared at my locker.

That move incensed Flanagan more. "Don't look away from me, asshole, when I'm talking to you." He shoved me so hard, I fell off the bench into my locker door, cutting the top of my head in the process. I immediately got off the floor and leapt upon the bench and jumped onto Flanagan, and then I proceeded to punch him all over the head. But my punches added up to nothing more than mosquito bites. Flanagan shook me off so hard, I wound up being slammed into the lockers this time with my whole body.

One of the gym teachers, Paulsen, a tall, gray-haired fellow, came rushing over to check out the commotion. "What the hell is going on here?" he demanded. Then he saw me lying on the floor, bleeding from the head, and I know I was bleeding from the back as well. I felt underneath my shirt where there was a stinging sensation at the center of my back. It was moist. I looked at my hand and knew I must have landed on something sharp or jagged when I had been launched against the locker doors.

Steve Greco, the best weightlifter in my class, stuck up for me. "This fat kid starts hitting this kid for no reason and tosses him into a locker."

Paulsen knew me from a couple of gym classes I had taken with him in the past. "All right, Greco, I saw the whole thing myself. Are you alright, McPherson?"

I nodded, a bit dazed from the action.

"Wait a minute," Flanagan protested. He jumped on me, and he wouldn't get off me, so I had to shake him off."

"You pushed him off the bench, right into the locker. Why don't you try pushing me, asshole!" Greco shouted.

Paulsen quickly interjected. "All right, enough of this! *You,*" he said, pointing to Flanagan, "are going to the dean's office. And *you,*" he pointed to Greco, "keep your damn mouth shut."

Paulsen sent me over to the nurse's station, where the nurse, a middle-age lady along the likes of Aunt Jane, washed my wound, cleaned my head wound and bandaged it.

"What gets you into you kids? Why do you fight so much?"

I was a bit irritated by the questioning, and I told the nurse so. "He shoved me into a locker for no reason. That's why I'm cut up!"

She didn't say anything after that. I didn't expect her to. Another adult who assumes the worst about all teenagers, as if I had caused the fight.

I arrived late into Mrs. Welsh's class. She didn't give me any grief, seeing the bandage on my forehead. She did ask what happened and I simply answered that I had tripped and fallen in gym class. I didn't want to get into any specifics with her or in front of the gaping class.

Brenda was another story. Before the class started, she was up at the front of the room and I was already at my seat. She gave me an incredulous, "What happened this time?" look. I wasn't in the mood for this, and I just wanted to get the class over and done with.

We were analyzing poems. I just hated poetry with a passion, and all I could think about was Flanagan. How I wanted to place a few well-chosen kicks to his face. I wondered what was happening to him at that moment. Was the dean suspending him?

Those 40 minutes in Brenda's class seemed to last forever. But I didn't feel like filing out with the rest of the kids; otherwise I would get the questions of "What happened to you?" all over the bus.

Better to wait and head out to Hylan Boulevard, where I would catch a regular city bus with working-class Joes and Janes heading home. The only catch was having Brenda stop me and ask what she could do for me.

It also seemed very ludicrous to me that this woman would be so concerned when after this semester, I would be a distant memory in her mind.

"Hey, young man," Brenda called out as the bell rang. "Come talk to me."

I shuffled over and she asked me what I predicted: "What in the world happened this time?"

My reply belied my irritation. "A weight fell on top of my head in gym class. Why do you care, Brenda?"

"After six months of seeing you practically everyday and knowing more about your life than I do with most people, how can I not care?"

"After this semester, you'll forget all about me."

"You really believe that, hon?"

"That's how it goes, doesn't it?"

"Why does it have be that way with me?"

"You're a teacher and you see lots of kids every semester. Do you see still see every one of them?"

"Of course I don't, but there are some who still remain special to me. You would be one of them."

"I find that hard to believe.

"You are so cynical, my dear. Don't you remember what I said on your documentary," she said, as she placed her hand on my shoulder. "You are without a doubt my favorite. I have done more for you than any other student. You're like a brother to me, and I'm always watching over your back, trying to keep you out of trouble." Then she added with a laugh: "It hasn't been easy."

"This is all going to be over soon," I firmly stated.

"Does it have to be?" Brenda asked. "You could keep in touch if you wanted to. I know I will. True friends never leave you. They will always love you and never go away.

"I appreciate that. I want to keep in touch." That was a really nice statement about friendship.

"Very good. Now that we have that out of the way, can you tell me what happened?"

"I already told you. A weight fell on me."

"Roddy, this is me you're talking to. When you're distracted as you were in my class right earlier, something happened. Now what was it?"

I told Brenda the tale of Flanagan, and all she could do was shake her head in disbelief. "Oh my God, you poor thing! It's as if you have a "kick me" sign on the your back, but it's invisible to all but the jerks."

"I really want to leave school," I stated. "I'm not going to get through this."

"Roddy, tough it out. You have just one week of classes, then it's the regents. You're almost there."

It has been said too many times, but what would I have done without her support?

As I expected, the other kids asked me about Flanagan. Flanagan, as it turned out, was suspended. Paulsen had seen the whole incident unfold, and I was absolved of any wrongdoing.

Brenda Visits the Record Store

The thermostat was kicking into 90 degrees outside. Summer was here and it wasn't even officially June 21 yet. It was steamy in the record shop, and I think I did just as much sweating as I did during weight-training class, if not more. You still had a trickle of NYU students who were taking summer classes, and a majority of Rob's business came from that end. Not as much business like there had been before the end of the regular college semester in May, but still good enough for Rob to get by. After the end of July was when it would become totally dead for over a month, since there were no classes held at all and visiting students went back home. I kept telling Rob he should invest in an air conditioner, but the fool would not spring for one. "I can't afford it, man. Would you like it to come out of your salary?"

I was still hurting over Erika. It wasn't as bad as a few weeks back, but the heartache was lingering. Rob was hurting as well. We weren't saying much to each other and it wasn't the same as it used to be. Maybe in time it would change.

I had never expected Brenda Moriarty to visit the record shop in a million years, but she kept her promise of a few months ago. She was embracing the summer, casually dressed in a black tank top, white dungarees and black sandals. Her hair was slicked back with a white sweatband around it. Damn, she was hot, and Rob, friggin' snake that he was, was leering at her.

"Hey, hey Roddy. How are ya?" Brenda asked cheerfully.

I was pleased to see her. Even though I saw her every day, I could never get sick of her, and I knew the closeness would never be the same after this semester.

"What brings you to this hot box?" I asked.

"I keep my promises, and I needed to take a day for myself. Just hang out in the city, take it nice and slow. It is hot today, but I lived in Florida for a few years, so the hot weather doesn't bother me too much."

Rob interjected. "Hey, Roddy, aren't you going to introduce me to your friend?"

"Oh, Brenda, this is my boss, Rob Petrowski. Rob, this is my English teacher, Brenda Moriarty."

"Well, this is cool. I didn't believe Roddy when he told me how pretty you are. Usually, teachers are frumpy old hags. You're far from it."

Brenda flashed her winning smile. "Why, thank, you. It's really nice to meet you. I heard a lot about you. And I'm sorry to hear about your employee Erika. I had her as a student in one of my writing classes. She was really a nice girl."

"Yeah, thank you," Rob said low. "Me and Roddy still can't believe it. You think you could get over this, but I can't."

"It's never easy. I hadn't seen her in a while, but I remember her and the news of her death tore at me."

I excused myself from the counter and went to the bathroom. The waterworks followed and never mind Rob's "I couldn't get over it." I hated that feeling of having your heart ripped out. I just wish we could never talk about Erika, not for a while.

I turned on the cold water faucet and put my face underneath the cool liquid, slicking my hair back. After five minutes, I came out and I could hear Brenda stating gently to Rob, "Watch over him. He really is a good kid. He's like a brother to me."

"I will," Rob affirmed.

That conversation bit confused me. Was Brenda going somewhere?

They noticed me coming out of the backroom. "Oh, there he is," Brenda remarked. "I guess he needed to cool down. Are you okay, Roddy?"

"I'm good," I said. "Are you going on a vacation?"

"Well, my mom lives down in Florida, and I'm going to go down there after this semester for a month. I'm really needing a break."

Who could blame her? The woman oversaw her regular schedule of classes, put on a free writing workshop for four students and attended classes on her own, working her way toward her master's. Was it any small wonder that she needed a break?

"Hey, did you ever listen to *A Trick of the Tail* like I asked you to?" Brenda inquired.

"No, I never did. I preferred Peter Gabriel, and as good as Phil Collins was, I never found him as interesting as Gabriel. Gabriel had that otherworldly quality, and his weird imaginative sense of storytelling appealed to me.""You have to listen to it, Roddy. It's really that good. Trust me on this. There's still a copy left in the bin. I'm buying this one to…"

"…No, you're not," Rob said. "You can have it for free."

Brenda was mortified. "No, I can't let you do that. This is your business…"

"…Don't worry about it. You're a friend of Roddy's, and any friend of Roddy's is a friend of mine."

"That is so sweet, but remember, you still have to watch over my buddy when I leave for Florida." Brenda winked to me as she said this.

"Oh, don't worry. I'll take care of him," Rob said.

You fuckin' pothead, I thought to myself. You could barely take care of yourself; how in the hell are you going to watch over me?

"It was great meeting you, and thank you for the free album. I had this in college, but a roommate of mine never gave it back. I haven't listened to this in seven years. Roddy, be safe, and I'll see you tomorrow."

The friendly teacher disappeared into the daylight outside. Rob was impressed.

"I can see how you really like her. She's really pretty, but she's also a very nice person."

"I can only hope I meet a girl like her one day."

"That would be so cool," Rob concurred.

"Weren't you ever married?" I asked.

"Long time ago, my man. It didn't work out. I was more concerned about being in a band than I was in a relationship. The band never worked out, and I wish I could get her back."

"Have you tried to look for her?"

"I wouldn't know where to look. Last I heard, she was out in California someplace."

"You should look for her," I urged.

"If only I knew where. Look how hard it is for you to find that Puerto Rican chick."

"Thanks for reminding me, Rob." Now I felt more depressed than ever before.

The Dream That Was Too Good

Brenda's writing workshop was out on the lawn in Silver Lake Park. Only one more week was remaining with the writing quintet, and Brenda was finalizing matters.

"Okay, next week, it's our last class. I'm going to have you do an assignment for me this time. Tell how you felt about your experience regarding the class. Did you enjoy it, or did you hate it?"

"We know we didn't hate it," Latiesha chimed in.

"All right, but if there is something that you didn't like about the class, tell me."

"Well, the teacher was a pain in the ass," I joked.

"Oh, please!" Brenda playfully shoved me. "You never had such a good time in a class."

I went home that Sunday feeling uplifted. Belonging to that writing group really improved my mood, and as a tribute to Brenda I played *A Trick of the Tail* from Genesis. I always loved *The Lamb Lies Down on Broadway*; the themes of alienation always struck me. But Genesis' first album with Phil Collins as lead singer impressed the hell out of me. Nothing but great songwriting with exemplary playing and solid vocal performances by Phil Collins. Is this the same man who would later sing pap such as "Sussudio"? What in the hell happened to him over the years? How did he degenerate into singing music for housewives? "Ripples" was one gorgeous track whose melody stayed with me, particularly the middle section where Banks and Hackett are playing off each other. It's a very touching instrumental section that adds to the song's poignancy. I couldn't wait to express my feelings to Brenda about the album and thank her.

I had the best dream in a long while that night, and what a change it was from those nightmares that resulted from the muggings and beatings. I was in Brenda's apartment watching the intro to the ABC Saturday night movie. It was the same intro they had used for my favorite 4:30 movie when I was smaller. I was nostalgic for things '70s-ish a few years before it became in vogue, and this was one of them. Brenda came out of her bedroom wearing nothing but a men's shirt, unbuttoned to the point where you could see the top of her breasts. The here and now definitely took my mind off '70s nostalgia. She sat next to me on the couch and started stroking my cheek.

"Why are we kidding ourselves, Roddy? You have a major crush on me, and I find you extremely attractive. You're young, but you're wise beyond your years. And you can definitely take care of yourself."

"You never said that before," I sputtered.

"I guess I changed my mind," she said while still stroking my face.

"I don't think we sh..."

"...Shut up," Brenda said. She proceeded to lock lips with me, and I felt her tongue swirl in my mouth.

Brenda continued to hold onto my mouth with hers. She was taking my breath away, and she released only after what seemed an eternity.

She smiled. "Now tell me you have never felt anything for me before."

I couldn't help myself. I stripped down my pants, exposing my dick. I was rock hard, and that fact wasn't lost on her.

"Oh, my, aren't we well-endowed?" she commented.

I leapt on top of her and ripped off her shirt, exposing her nubile body. Brenda was not resisting my lust. I plunged my dick into her hot hole and we rocked, two bodies that were glistening with sweat as we steamed up one another on the couch.

Brenda was moaning. "Oh my God, don't stop. This feels so fuckin' good."

I grabbed her ample breasts while rocking. And I was feeling euphoric to the point where I couldn't see straight. But I was worried about pulling out of her before I could ejaculate into her. I barely managed to do so, the hot white liquid exploding all over her breasts.

Brenda welcomed that liquid explosion. "Ohhhhh, that warm, creamy, man lotion feels so good." My euphoria ended when I awakened to the darkness of my room. No Brenda, just the four walls of my room, and the window overseeing New York harbor. The white hot liquid was all over me, and I had to go the bathroom to clean it up. It was a good dream, but did it have to be *that* good?"

The next day, I told my Brenda my enthusiasm about *A Trick of the Tail.* "I loved it."

"I'm glad. I listened to the album on Saturday night. It's one of my favorites."

I wondered how Brenda would react if I told her about my dream, but some things are better off left being unsaid.

A Change of Plans

On the following day, Brenda looked very downbeat, something I had never seen in her before. When the students were reading our personal reviews of musical albums, her mind wandered off and her gaze was looking out the window, the same behavior as my own when I was troubled. Her smile wasn't there, and the twinkle of the eyes were gone. Perhaps it was a bad day, and hell, she was entitled. When I read my review of *The Lamb Lies Down on Broadway*, an album I know she was enthusiastic about as well as I was, she didn't even blink her eyes. All I got was "Good job, Roddy."

It was pretty much the same thing the following day. One of the few other males in the class besides me, a metal head named Steve Boscoli, wrote a great review of Megadeath's *Peace Sells...but Who's Buying?* I loved the descriptions of ear-splitting thrash metal, but Brenda wasn't attuned to what was going on. When Steve finished, he had to get Brenda's attention.

"Hey, Ms. Moriarty, I'm finished."

Brenda snapped out of her trance. "I'm sorry, Steve. I was listening, and that's an excellent review. But ear-splitting thrash is not my cup of tea, thank you."

The class got a chuckle out of that one. But something was not right.

I came up to Brenda after the class and asked her what was wrong, that she didn't seem like herself.

"I'm okay, hon," Brenda reassured me, "but thank you for asking. I'm just feeling burned out with work and school. Like you, I can't wait until this semester is over. I really need a vacation."

"Can I come with you?" I asked. It's going to be a lousy summer."

"Awww... Why do you say that?"

"I have no friends left, except Rob, and he hasn't been the same since Erika died. I have no one else."

"What about Brian?"

"I haven't seen him in a couple of weeks. Is Christine going out with him still?"

"Oh, yeah, she keeps talking about it as if she was one of these high school girls here. I had to tell her to shut up about it and that I really didn't care to hear it."

"And he's still going out with Tabitha, although I haven't heard anything yet."

"So, what are your plans for summer?"

"I guess I'll work a lot, keep myself busy. I have nowhere to go."

"I have to level with you, Roddy, and can you promise not to say anything to anybody else about it?"

"Okay."

My mom has an inoperable brain tumor. She hasn't been feeling well for some time. The test results came back yesterday, and she only has six months to live." Tears started to well down Brenda's face.

I felt bad for even inquiring. "I'm sorry, I didn't know, and I was concerned because you weren't yourself. I'm really sorry, Brenda."

"Thanks, Roddy. I was going to tell you next Sunday along with the other kids, but now you know. Just keep it to yourself, okay?"

I was never one to give up secrets, and who the hell was I going to tell?

Brenda wept. "I may not be back in New York for a while. I have to stay down there and take care of her. She took care of me for many years; it's my turn to take care of her."

My heart sank. I had never met Brenda's mom, but I felt her daughter's sadness about her right now. And if her mom was anything like her daughter, she must be quite a person.

"I'm sorry if I wasn't so attentive to the reviews in this class," Brenda went on. "My heart is not in this right now."

That was understandable. I wouldn't care about music reviews either. "Why don't you cancel next week's class? I'm sure the others would understand."

Brenda demurred. "No, it wouldn't be fair to you guys. Besides, I need the class too. I can't brood in my apartment."

I went home feeling just as grief-stricken as when Erika died. I really felt terrible about Brenda's mom and I wished I could somehow have the gift of healing powers and prevent her mom from dying. I also wanted to put that smile back on Brenda's face. For all the happiness she gave me, I wish I could do that much for her, but I couldn't. I was also losing a friend. There was no way in hell I could keep in contact with her. She would have more important things to contend with than deal with a former student.

Anger and sadness engulfed me. Brenda's mom didn't deserve this. Why do terrible things have to happen to people who don't deserve them? It tore out my heart to see Brenda hurt like that.

Selfishness crept in too. Here was a friend, one of the best I'd ever had, and she had to leave because of circumstances. I couldn't blame her, but it had been such an arduous semester and this was another loss I had to endure. Brenda wasn't dying, but she would be gone for who knows how long.

And guilt came into the equation. The woman's mom was dying, and was it right for me to be a selfish jerk?

I viewed myself in the mirror in my bedroom. I didn't like myself for feeling this way and I didn't like myself at all. I took my left fist and drove it hard into the mirror, cutting it. The blood trickled down my hand, but I wasn't fazed. It did sting. Not leaving bad enough alone, I took my right fist and drove it into my right eye twice, really hard. I saw stars, and that eye stung immediately. I was finished with the self-flagellation, but my anger was running high. I took what was left of the mirror and smashed it to the floor. It broke into many jagged, splintering pieces. Not satisfied with the destroyed mirror, I took my clothes drawer and overturned it. The piece of furniture was heavy, but I managed to flip it over. I don't think I could ever have repeated that feat. Whatever pieces were on that drawer — pictures, pens, pencils, coins, various souvenirs — went scattering all over the room. I took my desk chair and flung it against the wall. It ricocheted so hard, it almost struck me, and I barely managed to dodge it. I fell to my knees and started to sob like a baby.

An hour later, Aunt Jane saw the aftermath of the carnage I wrought upon myself and the room. She was mortified and asked what had happened. "What in the devil? Did a burglar break in?"

"I trashed the room and I hit myself," I said.

"Why? Have you gone off the deep end? For what insane reason would ye hurt yerself? What has warped yer mind?"

I told my aunt about Brenda's mom dying and how she had to leave. I was angry and sad not only about Brenda's troubles but because I was losing my friend. "I don't have anyone anymore. Killian is never around, Erika is dead and my boss, Rob, is not the same."

Aunt Jane was saddened by the news of Brenda's mom. "Oh, that poor girl. That poor girl's mother. You know she has to go to Florida to take care of her; she can't help that."

"I know, and that's why I hurt myself and trashed my room, because I'm not a good kid." I started to break down again. For someone who never cried, I was crying a lot lately. It was way too much.

"You are a good kid. You are a very good kid. You're not a self-ish for wanting her to stay. I know what she has done for ye. She made you believe in yourself, and that person is hard to find in life. I'm glad she came along. Ye had no direction before this, but you'll be fine. But that poor girl, I should call her."

"No," I said. "I promised Brenda I wouldn't tell anyone else. She'll be pissed at me."

"Who will I tell, Roddy? I know I look like an old hen, but I'm not one."

I just sat on my bed, an ice pack over my eye and my hand band-aged. Within a half hour, Brenda walked into my bedroom.

"Oh, my God, Roddy," she exclaimed in horror when viewing me and the room.

"I know you didn't want me to tell anyone else, but she had to know why I trashed the room."

"I'm not mad at you at all, but you why did you hurt yourself?"

"I'm a selfish bastard. I feel guilty for wanting you to stay."

Brenda sat down next to me on my bed. "You're not being self-ish. You don't want me to go. I don't want to go. I'm starting to build up my career again, and I'm happy here. But I've got no choice, and it's the least I can do for her."

"I know that."

"But I want you to keep in contact with me. Write me when the spirit moves you, or give me a call. If I don't answer right away, I'll get back as soon as I can."

"You know I can't do that. I would feel weird."

Brenda put her arm around me. "I've always said you are family to me. I always want to know what you are doing with yourself."

I nodded. I needed that reassurance. It made me feel just a little better. Some friends just leave and forget about you. This woman seemed like the real deal.

The final week of those classes went by. Of course, I got asked about my black eye and cut-up hand. I just told the students and teachers who were interested the truth: I got into a fight with a kid from the outside, and you should've seen the other kid.

Corsi looked at me incredulously. "Are you making up for lost time, or are you mad against the world?"

If he knew the truth, he would have thought me crazy for sure.

A Hero Once Again

I was waiting for the N train to take me up to West 8th Street in the Village. It was already too muggy to take that walk from South Ferry. Although after a minute of waiting in that urine-smelling, rat-infested subway station, I wondered if it might have been better to walk after all. There were a few others waiting on the platform besides me, two elderly black men, one well-dressed young professional female who kept fanning herself with her hand, a Hispanic female in her 30s with her two young sons. And teetering on the edge of the platform was a young guy in his 20s, wearing black slacks and a white shirt. He appeared odd to me, performing a dance in the subway station, but then again, this was New York City. What would it be without quirky people?

The green lights on the track lit up, signaling that my train was coming in. All the while I was watching this guy, and wondering if I should tell him to move back so he doesn't get struck by the train. Wouldn't you know it, he fell down onto the track!

The well-dressed woman shrieked: "Oh my God!" I rushed over and saw the man lying on the tracks with foam coming out of his mouth. It looked as if he was having a seizure.

I immediately jumped down onto the tracks, provoking screams and shouts from the shocked onlookers. The train was coming down the tracks, and I could hear the honking of the horn. I was doing my best to get the man's lifeless body on my back in a fireman's carry. I struggled at first, but with strength from I-don't-know-where, I was able to hoist him onto my back. I carried him over to the platform as fast as I could, and the two old men on the platform took the lifeless body off me.

The train was just a few feet away, and it wasn't slowing down. I scrambled up to the platform as fast as I could and barely got out of the way of the express train. After just surviving an oncoming train with inches to spare, I collapsed to the platform as the heat and physical activity took their toll.

As it seemed to be the case for much of this year, I found myself in the emergency room of a hospital. This was St. Vincent's on 12th Street in the Village area. I found myself on a gurney in one of those tight cubicles with an IV giving me fluid. I don't remember what happened between the time I climbed up the platform and woke up in the hospital.

A nurse came in, Italian-looking, very pretty. She noticed that my eyes were open.

"Well, hi there. How are you feeling?"

I shrugged my shoulders and asked why was I there.

"You passed out from heat exhaustion in the subway terminal. I heard about what you did. That is incredible. Did you know that you are a hero?"

"A hero?"

"Yes, you saved a man who had an epileptic seizure. You pulled him off the tracks, and I heard the train was coming in. That was brave."

I didn't think of it as anything special at all. Someone had to do something at the time, and all I could think about was what happened to Erika. And then I thought, "Why couldn't someone have saved her like I did with this guy?" And damn it, if you wouldn't know it, tears leaked from my eyes again. If there was an award for crybaby of the year, it would have been given to me.

The hospital got in touch with my emergency contact at home, Aunt Jane. She came in a couple of hours later, stressed out of her mind. "Oh, my lord, Roddy," she expressed joyously when she discovered I wasn't marked up or bruised. She came over and hugged me tightly.

"And true to form," she started scolding me. "Boy, what in the hell is wrong with ye? Now ye have to rescue people off of subway tracks? Don't ye care at least one lick of ye life? Ye giving me gray hairs all the time, and now ye want me to have a heart attack? Jaysus, son, ye going to be the death of me."

I could only smile. I knew all that scolding was because she loved me. I would have been mad about it six months ago, but she was one of the few who genuinely cared about me. Hadn't she taken me in when I was orphaned? The hospital discharged an hour later. Bed space was a precious commodity, and they weren't keeping someone who healthy and able to walk out of there that day. Before I could walk out, the ER staff, nurses, aides and doctors gathered around my cubicle. They gave me a round of applause and cheers. That was really a spiritual lift for me, for someone who had always felt he was a pile of useless shit.

My aunt had gone off to get her car, and when the staff wheeled me out to the curb, there was a group of reporters from the various news networks around NYC to greet me. The camera flashes were quite blinding, and I remember the questions coming at me at rapid fire:

"How are you feeling?"

"What made you jump onto those tracks and rescue that man?"

"How old are you?"

"Is that the bravest thing you have ever done?"

I was still a little bit disoriented when I was wheeled out to Aunt Jane's car. Was this really happening? Thankfully, hospital security was there to drive a wedge between me and the reporters, allowing the nurse's aides and Aunt Jane to load me into the car.

I was loaded and Aunt Jane pulled away with the reporters and cameras behind us. "What a living circus," she muttered. "Do you realize yer a hero to everyone, again? That is the bravest or the stupidest thing you have ever done, but I'm proud of ye son, I really am."

Throughout all the excitement, I forgot I was supposed to be in work that day. I told Aunt Jane about this, and she quickly dismissed that notion.

"Ye not working today. Ye just got out of the hospital. Yer going to go home and rest. Ye have all summer long to work if ye like."

"Does Rob know? Did you call him?"

"Will ye forget about yer boss! I'm sure he called home and if he did, ye call him back and tell him to turn on the news. He can figure out what happened."

When we arrived at our home, we found a couple of news vans outside.

"Good heavens, ye got be kiddin'. How in the devil did they know where we live?" Aunt Jane groaned.

If you have a nose for news, you know where to go. That's why I couldn't be a news reporter. It was too intrusive for my liking.

A pretty reporter from WNBC came up to me. "Hey, Roddy, would you mind answering a few questions?"

Aunt Jane rushed to the other side of the car. "Godsakes, leave him alone. He has to get his rest. Come back another time, please."

"But I just want to ask him a few questions," the woman protested.

"Okay, can ye reckon he can call ye at home."

"Well, we don't do things like that, Mrs. McPherson. We don't give out our personal phone numbers."

"And we don't give out our home address either. But someone gave it to ye. I didn't tell ye to come, now go home!"

The reporter was left looking stunned in her tracks as we went inside the house.

"This is unbelievable," my aunt went on. "I hope this isn't going to be like this for the rest of the day. Go take a shower, laddie. Clean yerself up a bit and just watch TV."

The cold running water never felt so good as I cleaned off that subway grime from the tracks. My body temperature cooled down rapidly.

The baseball game of the week was on NBC. Yanks versus Orioles. Always the Yanks or the Mets. Why not the Phillies or the previous year's champs, the Minnesota Twins? Nevertheless, I was too weary to channel surf, so I tried to settle down to watch some baseball. The TV and the humming of the air conditioner failed to drown out the ringing of the house bell or the phone. My aunt was beside herself: "Can't a person get some peace on a Saturday afternoon? This is insane!"

We had purchased a new phone with an answering machine unit, and my aunt always screened the calls. Nobody was leaving messages, and my aunt figured it must be the media. And when she took a peek through the curtains, the media circus had grown from one news van to about twenty, all on our block.

"Heaven and hell," Aunt Jane gaped, "it's a living circus out there."

We weren't going to get any peace, not until I answered some questions. "Aunt Jane, maybe if I just answer a few questions, perhaps they'll leave us alone. What do you think?"

"Ye probably right. Go on, then. Get it over with."

I opened the door and all those amazing bulb flashes just bounced off my face. It was intense. And there was a lot of shouting from the reporters.

In situations such as these when I had to address people, I was nervous. But the tiredness engulfing me made me forget my fear of speaking in front of many people.

"I'm really tired," I began. "It's been a long day, but I'll answer a few questions. That's all I can do."

"Roddy," a female voice called out. "How does it feel to be a hero?"

"I'm no hero. Cops and firemen are true heroes. They do this everyday and get little money," I answered.

"But you're an ordinary citizen. Very few people risk their lives to save a life in front of an oncoming train. What you did was extraordinary!"

I thought about it a moment, and yeah, it was ballsy. "I guess."

"Are you normally this brave?" a male reporter called out.

"No, I'm a coward. This is the first brave act I did," I answered, forgetting what I had done for Erika a couple of months back.

Maureen Steinhagen, the lovely reporter from the *Staten Island Advance* who interviewed me at the time of that holdup with Erika reminded me and the reporters of my previous heroism. Then she added: "You should become a policeman or firefighter. Any plans in those field of endeavors after you graduate?"

"No, I'm not cut out to be anything like them. Those fields are not for me."

"The person whose life you saved is going to be fine. How do you feel about that?"

I was relieved. "Pretty good."

"What do you plan to do after high school?"

"Go to film school."

"How do you feel about this being a good news story? In New York City, there's always bad news. But you provided people with good news. How does that make you feel?"

"Good, I guess."

Afterward, I said, "It's been along day. Excuse me." Then all those news crews, seemingly satisfied with what they had, broke up for the day.

And later that night, I was the top story on the newscast. But more importantly, I was glad that the person I rescued in the subway tunnel was going to be fine. A gent by the name of Steve Korenski, a Wall street stockbroker. Probably a yuppie. I hated yuppies; they seemed like a self-absorbed, self-centered lot. But no one deserves to get run over by a subway train — unless you wanted to count the piles of scum who had left me for dead, like my muggers back in February.

It was amusing watching myself on the tube answer those reporter's questions, but I could do well to change the sound of my voice.

A call came in later from Brenda: "Oh my God, Roddy, did you really do that? That is so brave. I'm really so proud of you."

"Thanks, but I'm not a hero."

"Oh, will you stop being so modest? You are a hero — face it."

"It's weird," I volunteered. "I don't feel heroic. I still feel like me."

"Well, you are very special," Brenda pointed out. "And yes, you deserve all the good comments that people are saying about you. So roll with it."

"Thanks."

"Listen, I wouldn't blame you for not coming tomorrow if you weren't up to it."

"No, I am coming tomorrow," I said. "Your class means a lot to me, and I'm not missing it."

"It's up to you, Roddy, it's up to you. But if you don't come, I understand. Try to rest up, and once again, I'm proud of you. I really am."

I had every intention of attending that last workshop, but there were some obstacles to navigate, namely some lingering reporters milling about the front of the house, and so I had to escape through the back yard into the neighbors' yard. Aunt Jane had called my neighbors and told them what was happening. The Gigantes. They were an elderly couple and really nice people.

I arrived at the park, and the class was sitting on the blanket Brenda usually provided along with her homemade cookies and iced tea, of course. The gang gave me a hero's welcome by clapping.

"There he is," announced Brenda proudly. "My hero."

I was embarrassed by such a display. I didn't feel like a hero. Isn't a hero supposed to feel like Superman? How come I wasn't flying in the air with a red cape?

"Aww, he's blushing. That is so cute," exclaimed Brenda.

"Stop it already!"

"Stop what?" Brenda stood up to give me a huge hug. "People are going to be talking about you for a while. It was so selfless; it's incredible."

Latiesha chimed in: "Brenda is right. That is so brave. But weren't you scared?"

Of course I was. I was still shaking. I showed my hands, which really were shaking, but I was probably keyed up from all this excitement.

"Sit down, hon," Brenda said. "I'm glad you could come. It wouldn't be the same without you. Now I already told them about my mom. I may not be back here for a while, but I want all you to keep in touch with me. That would mean a whole lot."

The rest of the gang had been crying. I could see their watery eyes.

"No one helped us like you did," Lucia said. "That's what makes it sad."

Brenda hugged her from the side. "And I will always be here to help. Never hesitate to call me. Don't be afraid, any of you."

We all read our assessments of the class. Latiesha spoke about how Brenda would give her a supportive hug after English class when telling her details about her family. Tim read about how Brenda made it seem okay for a freak like him to exist.

"You're not a freak, Tim. You're a young man who has a speech impediment, but it's getting better. The people who laugh at you are the freaks," Brenda pointed out.

Lucia talked about how Brenda's smile was contagious. "You made us feel really good about ourselves and that we counted for something."

"You, do, hon. You four were very troubled kids, and I tried to do whatever I could to make you feel good about yourselves. I know you all have hard lives, but I hope I provided a diversion from what was going on."

It was my turn, and I pointed out how Brenda instilled confidence in ourselves as writers and that we could take on any assignment. The "hon" and "sweetie" terms of endearment that she called us would be missed severely. "It was a hard year," I said, "but you made it bearable."

"You're going to be fine. You proved that yesterday," Brenda reassured me.

That class went on for two hours. It was a love fest spearheaded by one of the best people I have ever known. If the reporters could have seen what I saw, wouldn't they be honoring Brenda Moriarty. Kind words and a heartwarming smile go a long way.

Well, we did honor Brenda with a $50 gift certificate to Macy's. All five of us chipped in. She was really touched by the gesture: "This is so unbelievable. You did not have to do this!"

It was Latiesha's idea: "We wanted to." And she could have added: "How could we not?"

Meeting the Mayor

The media attention was enormous from this event. My puss was plastered all over the newspapers of the nation and even in other parts of the world. People must have been crying for a good news story all the while, and I had never thought in my wildest dreams I could ever be the main topic of such a story.

I got two invitations. The first one was to City Hall. The second was for *The Tonight Show* with Johnny Carson out in L.A. The summer was looking better than I had figured. Well, the beginning part of it anyway.

The week of the regents followed that workshop. In between the history and English examinations, I was able to fit in that ceremony at City Hall with the mayor. I know it sounds rather hokey, but I enjoyed meeting a public official. Aunt Jane was a huge fan of Mayor Koch and was charmed by him.

"How'm I doing?" the mayor asked my aunt his signature question.

"Yer doing a good job, Mr. Mayor, but ye got to clean up that crime better. Roddy has been a victim of a mugging and a robbery."

"You're kiddng?" asked the mayor incredulously.

"Oh, I'm serious," my aunt went on. "Even Staten Island has its problems. People get scared, and with good reason."

"I'm doing all I can, Mrs. McPherson. I'm not happy about it either, but we're trying. I'm putting more police out there and hopefully things will improve."

"Thanks for standing up for working people like us. You made this city bearable for us."

"My pleasure, Mrs. McPherson."

The mayor turned his attentions to me: "And you, young man, you are one courageous gentleman. You should be proud of yourself. The city and myself see you as a hero."

I kept hearing that word "hero." It was starting to grate a bit. But you can't stop people from feeling what they want to believe.

What was important that day was that I met the man whose life I saved in that subway, Steve Korenski. He seemed to be a really nice guy, not full of arrogance and attitude like most yuppies seemed to be.

"I have to thank you for saving my life. You really are a brave kid. I don't know if I could ever repay you."

I would hope someone would do the same for me if I ever fell onto the tracks. "Don't worry about it. You don't owe me anything."

"No, I want to do something. Are you a sports fan?"

"Yeah, I like baseball."

"Are you a Mets fan?"

"No, I'm a Phillies fan."

"Really. Are you from Philly?"

"No, it's just the team I happened to like growing up as a kid. Mike Schmidt, Pete Rose, Steve Carlton, Tug McGraw. Those guys were phenomenal."

"Yeah, those were some teams. Look, I can get you tickets to Shea when the Phillies come into town. I work for Merrill Lynch. We have a box over there at the stadium. And you can check out a real team, the Mets."

"Those drug addicts aren't going anywhere," I scoffed. "Strawberry, Gooden, Hernandez?"

"Aww, they're great. They will win it all this year. Go see a real team this year. I'll give you a couple of tickets for a corporate box. Your team is horrendous. Even Schmidt is terrible."

It was true. The Phillies were tanking big time. Steve was right.

Mike Schmidt, closing in on retirement, was not faring well — and he's all they had left. It was a sad time to be a Phillies fan.

"Seriously, Roddy, anytime you want Mets-Phillies tickets, let me know."

The City of New York had set up an awards ceremony for me. To my aunt's astonishment, and my own, they awarded me $20,000 for my good Samaritan act. I knew exactly where that money was going: film school. That was a question mark no more. Is it wrong to take money for saving someone's life? Perhaps, but I needed this money for my dream. Tuition at these film schools, such as UCLA, wasn't cheap, and it's not like I was wasting it. My aunt would be on my back to be wise with it anyhow.

The press conference was more of the same — "were you ever scared" and "do you feel heroic" kind of questions — but a couple of new ones made the circuit this time. "How do the kids feel about you at school?" was the first one. I answered that I had been shy and not known, but now I was. "Better late than never, right?"

The press laughed at that one. And another was, "What are you planning to do with the money?"

"Go to film school," I answered quickly. "It's always been a dream of mine."

Later my aunt and I went off to lunch with the mayor and his aides to Tavern on the Green. The mayor was nice enough to chauffer his limo out to us on the Island, and he extended that courtesy to us on our trip home. It was nice riding in style. I could see how a man could get used to this.

The restaurant was okay, nothing really spectacular. My aunt's roast beef dinner was far superior, but it was a nice day out, and it was a treat for Aunt Jane as well. I know she enjoyed the notoriety of being known as the woman who helped raise this hero up.

On the way back, she let me in on something.

"Look, Roddy, ye should save some of that money. I'll give ye $10,000 for tuition. I spent the last 10, 11 years working toward your education. Put half of it in your account. Ye need to save that. It's not really that much money, and it can go rather fast if you are not careful."

I was floored. "But I thought you couldn't afford to send me."

"I'm only giving ye some. If it was just another community college, I could, but this is yer dream, and ye deserve to be happy. You've been through so much." Aunt Jane touched my face with her right hand as she said this.

I was moved, and this almost made up for the gloom I felt regarding Brenda's soon-to-be absence.

During the days I took my exams, acquaintances and kids I had never talked to came up to me and congratulated me on my heroism. I remember a group of girls waiting out in the hallway for their friends during the exams smiling and waving to me: "Hey, we saw you on television. Congratulations."

Even jock types were coming up to me and saying, "Nice going, man."

"Awesome" and "That is so cool" were the other expressions I heard throughout those days.

Louise Meyers, that nice girl who had known me since the eighth grade and who never made any snickering comments, and had always treated me with respect, came up to me and gave me a hug. "That is so incredible, Roddy. You are amazing."

I shrugged my shoulders, but my head was starting to swell a bit. "It was really nothing."

"You're the talk of the whole school. But you deserve it. You really are a sweet guy, and it's time people knew that. You were always better than those jerks who used to torment you."

"Thanks, Louise, and thanks for never making fun of me back then."

"You're welcome. Hey, I noticed you have your yearbook. Why don't you let me sign it and you sign mine?"

Too bad she had a boyfriend.

Graduation Day

The big day had arrived. This was the first rite of passage into my adulthood, graduating high school. But damn it was hot that day! Wearing a suit with a green gown on top didn't make for a comfortable experience. I wondered if it was really necessary to be at this ceremony. With my aunt's prodding, I decided to get a haircut for the ceremony. It was still long in the back, but cut shorter on top in the frame of a mini-mullet. But I wondered why I even bothered. I wasn't receiving awards this year. What was the purpose?

They held the ceremony out on the football field, where everyone could enjoy sweltering. I realize I'm crying about it, but I hate hot weather. They had a canopy for the teachers to sit on, and where the students would go to get their awards at the center of the field, shaded of course, while the peasants sweltered in the sun.

Brenda Moriarty was there, outfitted in a sundress and a straw hat, looking radiant. She got a big cheer from the students, especially those who had her, and some whistles as well.

I wasn't expecting to get any awards. Let's face it, you had to be an Arista student to get above 90. I had that average running in history and English, but not above. In a way, it was a bit unfair, but be as that may, this was my day of emancipation form this lousy hellhole. When Brenda took the microphone to announce an award, cheers and wolf whistles rang out again. Brenda was a good sport and she didn't seem offended. But I wondered if these idiots hooting at her would cheer for her if they knew of her sexual orientation.

"It gives me great pleasure to announce this award. These two students were in my classroom, and I've gotten to know them very well. This citizenship award goes for outstanding community service.

"The first award winner is Latiesha Wilkins. Latiesha volunteered in her community many afternoons and weekends at Bayley

Seton Hospital. She truly is an example of giving back to her community. Come up here, Latiesha and get your award."

I was happy for Latiesha. She was a nice person, and she got a huge round of applause from all the parents sitting out in the bleachers. But the applause from the students was scattered, except for the black students. I stood up and clapped along with the black students.

There were white students seated next to me who looked at me quizzically, but I didn't care if only the black segment of the graduating body were on their feet. She was a friend, so why not join in?

Latiesha went up to the podium and received a huge hug from Brenda as the certificate was presented. After the audience quieted own, Brenda started again. "Like I said before, we are honoring two students. In the last two weeks, many of us on Staten Island and New York City have gotten to know this young man as the hero of that incident in the subway, where a gentleman fell to the tracks while suffering a seizure. It took incredible bravery and selflessness to do what this person did. I know I couldn't have done that," Brenda joked to some laughs in the audience.

"Please," I thought to myself. "You of all people would throw a person out of the way and let yourself get struck."

"The second citizenship award goes to Roddy McPherson." The students and the family members of the graduates in the bleachers burst into wild applause and cheers. It was incredible getting cheered, and it was such a good feeling to get swept away like that.

I bounced up to the canopy area, where I was greeted by Brenda with a hug and a kiss.

"Congratulations. You deserve it."

Latiesha and I hugged as well. It had been a trying year for both of us. I told her that she deserved hers more. I felt bad that the cheers from the students seemed to be racially motivated.

"No, that was great what you did," Latiesha countered. "You deserve yours."

And we went back to our seats with more cheers cascading around us in the hot open air.

After the tassels were thrown in the air, it was all over. Four years, just like that. But at least it was a happy ending.

Last Day of School

This day was just to pick up our report cards. I figured I would ride the bus one last time as a tribute. And I needed to say goodbye to a friend.

After graduation day, Brenda had celebrated alongside Latiesha and her mom, which I thought was really sweet. Brenda stated that she wanted to see me on the last day of school. I came by Room 304 in the North end of the building, where Brenda was sitting on the edge of her desk, outfitted in jeans, pink T-shirt and sandals, casually signing yearbooks and wishing students good luck.

After all this business of wishing her students well and saying goodbye to her colleagues, Brenda offered me a farewell lunch.

"Let's get a couple of slices, Roddy. I'm hungry."

We hopped in her car and went off to a pizzeria in my neighborhood, Villa Marino. I found it odd that an older woman would want to spend time with me, and it was weird viewing her as a friend sometimes. "Aren't you afraid of what people think when you are around students?"

"And what's that?"

This was uncomfortable as hell. "You know, they think that you and I might be, you know…"

Brenda smiled slightly. "Getting it on?"

"Yeah."

She chuckled at that one. "I can't help what people think, and I really don't care. It's very sad people have that mindset as if something illicit is going on. That is really sick thinking and in no way would I have sexual relations with a student. I'm sure there are some teachers who have done that, but I find that disturbing. I have spent individual time with other students because sometimes students need more than what they get in the classroom. Maybe they need a mentor, someone to help them along in life. Mrs. Kaplan, the English teacher I had in high school, was definitely my mentor, and she used to spend time with me after school, and with a few others as well. She held unofficial writing workshops with students."

There was a brief pause. "And you are no longer my student, Roddy. That phase is over. We are friends, and always will be."

"You really mean that?"

"Always," she reassured me by touching my arm.

Brenda returned to the subject of work. "There will probably come a time where I won't be able to do this, and I'll have to cut back on these extracurricular activities. Perhaps I'll settle down with someone, adopt kids. I know I can't keep up the pace forever like I did this year with the workshop."

Perhaps, but I was sure glad she was my teacher. Those workshops helped me, because the 40 minutes of class time was just never enough. My writing skills benefited enormously. I told her about an invitation I received for *The Tonight Show*. I was going to be Johnny Carson's guest, and my aunt was going along as well.

"Oh my God, that is so wonderful. You really made the big time. That is going to be so cute. I can't wait to see that!"

"I wish I could help you move, but I can't. We leave tomorrow. I'll be on the show the following day, the 30th."

"That's okay. My brother and a few of his buddies are helping me, along with Christine and your friend Brian. I'm sorry his ex took it out on you. You didn't deserve that."

Yes, Tabitha. I had seen her two days earlier at the Staten Island Mall. She had caught Killian cheating on her and wanted to know if I knew anything about it. I'm not a good liar and admitted that I had known.

"Why didn't you tell me?" she yelled in exasperation.

What could I say? "I felt it was none of my business."

"Well, it *was* your business, Roddy. I thought of you as a friend, but obviously you are not. You had my number; you could have called me. I guess you're not as heroic as people think you are."

That really hurt, and would you believe I would trade all that hero worship nonsense that was going on with me to have Tabitha's friendship back?

"Maybe I deserved it," I commented to Brenda.

"No, you didn't," Brenda reasoned. "She's upset, and I can't blame her. You were the closest target, but it wasn't fair of her to unload on you like that."

There was pause as we munched on our slices, but Brenda never let silent pauses carry on. "I want to give you something," she said. She produced a silver Celtic cross on a chain and gave it to me.

"It's not much, but I knew you would like it. You have Celtic heritage, so I figured it was a safe bet. Why don't you let me put it on you?"

Brenda stood up and clasped it around my neck. "Turn around so I can see it," she instructed. "Oh, that looks really good."

"Thanks, you didn't have to."

"I know I didn't have to; I wanted to. I hope you like it. And I also got you something else." She presented a registration receipt to a writing class.

"This is for a beginner's screenwriting class. You need another outlet besides your job."

I was floored by the women's generosity. "You did not have to that! I can't let you do this."

"It's paid for, Roddy. It's paid for."

I gave her a hug of my own. "You really are awesome. Can't you stay longer?"

"I wish I could, but remember, you're going to be fine. And keep in touch; otherwise I won't be happy with you."

Lunch ended. I insisted on paying, but Brenda wouldn't hear of it. "That's sweet, but you need to save your money," she cautioned me.

When Brenda took me home, she pulled in front of my house, and I really started to break down, knowing this was goodbye for real.

"Hey, hey," she said as she did her best to comfort me by embracing me, but she was failing, crying her own tears. "You don't think I'm going to miss all this?"

"Why do all good people leave?" I asked.

"I'm always here, Roddy. Please, pick up the phone and call me, anytime, any day."

"Do you mean that?"

Yes, I'm always your friend, no matter what."

"I'm afraid I'm a bother."

"You're not. Listen, I'll tell you what, I'll call you for your birthday at the end of the month, how's that?"

"I would love that. And Brenda?"

"Yes, dear?"

"I never tell too many people this, but I love you."

"The feeling is mutual, Roddy. I love you, too. You're family to me."

Our embraces unlocked, we bid our goodbyes, and off Brenda drove. And just like that, five months of closeness had come to an end. I wondered if I could ever meet a girl who could match her kindness and consideration. I fell in love with her because of those attributes.

I'll never forget the inscription she wrote in my yearbook:

"Roddy, best of luck in all your future endeavors. You truly are a gem. It was my pleasure having you as a student, and even a bigger pleasure having you as a friend. Please keep in touch. Love always, Brenda."

Aftermath

My aunt and I made the trip out to L.A., where we took in the sights of Hollywood, Disneyland and Venice Beach. The weather was warm, but there was none of that oppressive humidity like out in the east. I wished I could relocate out to California, but the living costs were just too much. Besides, I had to look out for Aunt Jane, and as long as she was alive, I wasn't going anywhere from NYC. I made the decision to attend the New York University. They had an excellent film studies program.

Johnny Carson and Ed McMahon were gracious guys. Carson asked me why I wanted to be a part of this crazy business called Hollywood. I just stated that "You have to be crazy to be in this business — that's why *you're* in it." And that got a laugh from the audience as well as from those two.

I managed to meet a couple of celebrities, Martin Sheen and Heather Locklear. Both of them were down to earth, gracious people, asking me for my autograph! I had enjoyed Martin Sheen's work in *Badlands* and *Apocalypse Now*. What a warm-hearted, wonderful guy. Locklear was simply gorgeous. But she wasn't stuck up at all. This was further proof besides Brenda that just because you were pretty didn't necessarily mean you were stuck up. She, along with Sheen, showed a genuine interest in my life and my career plans. My aunt liked her because she had a Scottish background. And what was amazing is that they both gave me the offer of help if and when I decided to come out to Hollywood to work in motion pictures.

The hero status wore off as I settled back into my life of working and taking the writing course. Linda Kaplan, the instructor, who was Brenda's mentor, was an extremely nice lady, sort of an ex-flower girl, but she wasn't Brenda. Still and all, she taught me how to refine my writing in regards to screenwriting. The days got hotter that summer. I sure wished I had a swimming pool. It was a sauna at the Record Den, despite it being a cellar. And Rob hired a new employee to replace Erika, a dweeb named Marcus Goodwin. Marcus was a precocious bastard, just a couple of years younger than myself, and he always had to express an opinion on music. The Stones are not what they once were. He was quite critical with the music I listened to, claiming Paul McCartney makes weak and embarrassing music as a solo artist. The Beatles are way over-rated. And the progressive music I loved such as Yes, ELP and Genesis, he characterized as boring, overindulgent and pretentious. If anyone was boring, overindulgent and pretentious, it was this nerd. He needed a good smack. For some weird reason, I started to call him Myron. "Oh, yes Myron, that's a good point." "Yes, Myron, you know what you speak of." He would get irritated and state, "My name is Marcus, or you can call me Marc."

"Okay, Myron, whatever you say."

One day, he blew up after I called him Myron for the hundredth time.

"Stop calling me, Myron, you asshole. My name is Marc. Marc! Are you dense?"

"Then stop acting like a conceited arrogant dick, and I'll call you by your proper name, fuckface!"

He went after me. I had been waiting for this moment. But before he could reach me, I knocked off his glasses and walloped him across the ear. That got him really pissed and he charged at me, his fists flailing wildly. We both fell to the floor in a heap, and it was a good thing Rob intervened, because we were ready to kill each other.

"Hey, stop this shit, right now, both of you!" Rob yelled. If the two of you can't get along, get out of the store and go home! I'll run this place without you two babies. I'm sick and tired of this shit, man! Roddy, stop antagonizing him! Marc, keep your opinions to yourself! We don't always want to hear it!"

We came to a truce where we didn't say anything at all to each other. I didn't have to work with him everyday, only on Saturdays mainly. But we learned to stay out of each other's hair.

I was resentful, because the kid wasn't Erika, and I wanted Erika back. Erika could be critical with the sounds I loved, but she did it in a joking manner and never took herself seriously.

Besides, she loved me as a friend, I loved her back, and this Marcus kid had no redeemable qualities as far as I was concerned. He had one of those nerdy side-parted '80s haircuts butchered in the back but long and floppy in the front. His tastes were mainly in the '80s punk scene, such as Black Flag, which didn't do it for me.

On one of my off days, I decided to go into Brooklyn and walk along the park on Shore Drive in Bay Ridge. It wasn't as humid as on previous days, so that helped. Why I chose Shore Drive, I just don't know. It was closer to where Erika lived, and I wanted to be near her.

A young girl sat on a bench, writing in a pad. Now, this was something I normally wouldn't have done, but I approached her and we started talking.

The girl removed her glasses. She had long dark hair, combed from the right side. Her skin tone was dark and her face was rather round, pleasant looking, very cute actually. And her smile was wide.

And she was dressed in white blouse, black slacks and pumps.

"Oh, I'm just taking notes about what I have to do for my church meeting later on," she said. "I work in a law office part time, which is why I'm all dressed up. I just got off work. Are you a writer?"

"Well, I want to be. I'm planning to go to film school. I'm going to write screenplays.

The girl had a light Spanish accent. "That's interesting." There was something about the girl I recognized. I knew her from someplace, but where? "You're a writer?" she asked.

"Well, it's nothing, and it's not important, is it?"

The girl frowned. "Why are writers not important?"

"Because all we do is entertain. We're not saving mankind."

"Entertainment is good," the girl pointed out. "People need entertainment to get away from their lives."

I nodded. But I still felt writers were inessential, especially compared with doctors. Whose lives were we saving?

She looked at me intently. "I know you from somewhere."

"Yeah, I was the kid who rescued that seizure victim in the subway."

The girl did a double take. "Oh, my God, Roddy? Roddy McPherson? I don't know if you remember me, but I'm Jasmine! Jasmine Flores."

Wow! Who would have thought of us meeting in a park in a chance encounter? What were the odds?

"Holy cow!" I jumped to my feet. I have been looking for you for so long. You wouldn't believe it."

She came over and hugged me. "How are you? Wow, this is so cool!" But then after the hug was broken, she gave me a forlorn look. "You just stopped writing, and I was so sad. Why, Roddy?"

I was the one who stopped the writing. Because at 7 years old, I was broken up about being separated from the Bronx, from Jasmine, and still traumatized from my mom's death. In Jasmine's case, when you see a person almost every day, and then you move far away, you never get to see the person so much, and her writing me would make me sadder and miss her more. I told Jasmine about this, and I told her about Brenda, and how that was so similar since she moved away.

"She seems like a nice person," Jasmine commented. "You should keep in contact with her. She cares about you a lot! And now that I met up with you, you're never going away from me now."

Jasmine explained that her family had moved out of the Bronx two years after my mom passed on and into Bay Ridge, where they had been ever since. Her parents were still living. She was a stone's throw away from the harbor, but I never knew it. All this time!

Jasmine revealed her plans for the future. She was going into social work after she graduated college the following year.

"I want to help people, especially kids. The world can be pretty dangerous. I have gone back to Highbridge, and there's a lot of poverty. A lot of good kids get swept into bad things, and you wish you could help them all, or at least most of them. I can only try."

But the world that day was a happy and safe one for both Jasmine and me. We talked for a few hours, two long-lost friends making up for lost time, not wanting to let the time pass so quickly. Getting out from underneath all the crap I had been through and meeting up with an old friend was the best reward I ever could have received.

Brenda was right when she stated, "True friends are like family. They always love you and never go away."

Made in the USA
Charleston, SC
08 September 2011